WALCH PUBLISHING

Daily Warm-Ups

PREFIXES, SUFFIXES, & ROOTS

Liza Kleinman

Level II

1   2   3   4   5   6   7   8   9   10

ISBN 0-8251-6050-2

Copyright © 2006

J. Weston Walch, Publisher

P.O. Box 658 • Portland, Maine 04104-0658

www.walch.com

Printed in the United States of America

Table of Contents

The *Daily Warm-Ups* series is a wonderful way to turn extra classroom minutes into valuable learning time. The 180 quick activities—one for each day of the school year—practice English/language arts skills. These daily activities may be used at the very beginning of class to get students into learning mode, near the end of class to make good educational use of that transitional time, in the middle of class to shift gears between lessons—or whenever else you have minutes that now go unused.

Daily Warm-Ups are easy-to-use reproducibles—simply photocopy the day's activity and distribute it. Or make a transparency of the activity and project it on the board. You may want to use the activities for extra-credit points or as a check on the English/language arts skills that are built and acquired over time.

However you choose to use them, *Daily Warm-Ups* are a convenient and useful supplement to your regular lesson plans. Make every minute of your class time count!

That's Bitter!

ace, aci, acri—roots meaning *sour* or *bitter*

Choose a word from the box below to complete each sentence. Write the word on the line.

acidity	acerbic	acrimonious	acrid

1. As the argument escalated, it grew more and more _____, until everyone said things they wished they hadn't.

2. Litmus paper indicates the _____ of a solution by turning red if the solution contains acid.

3. An _____ smell wafted in from the kitchen, where a pot of scorched sauce sat burning on the stove.

4. The reviewer was known for his dry wit and _____ commentary.

1

What's the Root? I

Each of the following words is missing the same root. Use the definitions to figure out the missing root. Then answer the questions that follow.

_____itate—to move; to stir things up

_____ent—someone or something that acts or effects change

_____enda—list of things to be done

2

1. What is the missing root? _____

2. What do you think it means? _____

Good and Bad

ben, bene, bon—roots meaning *good, well*

mal—root meaning *bad*

Choose the correct word to complete each sentence.

1. Thanks to the donation of our generous _____, our organization will be able to serve many more people this year.

   a. benefactor   b. malefactor

2. That was no accident—it was a purposeful, _____ act intended to wound the team's best player.

   a. benevolent   b. malevolent

3. To show its appreciation for its employees, the company will reward everyone with a _____ check this year.

   a. bonus   b. malady

Body Parts

Each of these roots describes a particular part of the body: *card, dent, man, ped, psych.*

Complete each sentence by writing in the correct root.

1. Regular visits to the _____ist will help maintain healthy teeth.

2. A _____io fitness routine gets the heart pumping quickly.

3. You propel a bicycle by using foot _____als to turn the wheels.

4. Years of _____ual labor had left his hands rough and scarred.

5. The movie was a complex _____ological thriller in which each character was well-developed and fascinating.

Now write the meaning of each root on the line.

6. *card:* _____

7. *dent:* _____

8. *man:* _____

9. *ped:* _____

10. *psych:* _____

4

Follow the Rules

crat, cracy, archy—roots meaning *rule*

Choose a word from the box below to complete each sentence. Write the word on the line.

aristocracy   oligarchy   democracy   monarchy

1. In a(n) _____, all citizens have a say in the government.

2. A(n) _____ is ruled by a king or a queen.

3. In a(n) _____, the nobility rule.

4. A country run by a small group of people is a(n) _____.

5. Now use two of the words from the box above in sentences of your own.

Keep Talking

locut, loqu—roots meaning *to talk*

Complete each sentence by filling in the missing roots.

1. A soli_____y is a speech given by one person.

2. A _____acious person talks a lot.

3. E_____ion is the art of speaking effectively in public.

4. An e_____ent speaker expresses herself well.

5. Circum_____ion is talking around something, or speaking evasively.

6. Can you think of any other words that contain these roots? List them below.

6

Daily Warm-Ups: Prefixes, Suffixes, & Roots

Life and Death

viv, vit—roots meaning *life*

mort—root meaning *death*

Match each word to its definition by writing the correct letter on each line.

___ 1. vivacious

___ 2. mortal

___ 3. vital

___ 4. mortician

___ 5. vivid

a. causing death, fatal

b. necessary for maintaining life

c. having a strong, bright, and lively appearance

d. full of lively spirit

e. undertaker

Making and Doing

Each of these roots means *to make, to do: fac, fic, fec, fect.*

Complete each sentence with a common word that contains *fac, fic, fec,* or *fect.*

1. A _____ is a place where goods are made.

2. Although the story sounded as though it could be true, it was a work of _____.

3. The best way to avoid becoming _____ with a cold is to wash your hands frequently.

4. Karen's good deed had a ripple _____. Her actions inspired other people to do good deeds, as well.

5. I will keep my opinion to myself, so as not to _____ your decision.

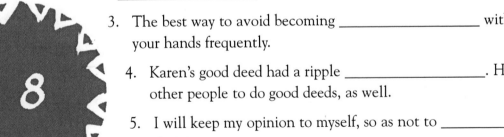

8

Number Roots

The following roots have number meanings:

dec—root meaning *ten*

cent—root meaning *hundred*

milli—root meaning *thousand*

Choose the correct root from the box below to complete each sentence. Write it on the line.

dec	cent	milli

1. A _____ury is a hundred years.

2. A _____meter is a thousandth of a meter.

3. The _____imal system is based on the number ten.

4. The United States celebrated its bi_____tennial in 1976.

5. A period of ten years is called a _____ade.

9

Daily Warm-Ups: Prefixes, Suffixes, & Roots

What's the Root? II

Daily Warm-Ups: Prefixes, Suffixes, & Roots

All of these words are missing the same root. Use the definitions to figure out what the missing root is. Then answer the questions that follow.

____ation—a calling; a job

e___ative—calling up, such as feelings or memories

equi___cal—having two sides; able to be interpreted in more than one way (literally, equal voices)

ad_____ate—somebody who supports, defends, or speaks for a cause

10

1. What is the missing root? _____

2. What do you think it means? _____

Daily Warm–Ups: Prefixes, Suffixes, & Roots

Scientific Roots

The following roots are found in scientific terms: *aero, geo, herbi, hydro, photo.*

Complete each sentence by filling in the missing root.

1. In _____graphy, we learn bout the earth's physical and cultural features.

2. A(n) _____cide is a product used to kill weeds.

3. The energy from the rushing waters of Niagara Falls is a source of _____electric power.

4. Plants use light to produce food in a process called _____synthesis.

5. For centuries, people have been fascinated by _____dynamics, designing gliders, wings, and flying machines with some success.

6. Now write the meaning of each root below or on a separate sheet of paper.

11

Being Born

nat—root meaning *born*

Choose the correct word from the box below to complete each sentence. Write the word on the line.

naturalized native supernatural international prenatal

1. It is very important that pregnant women receive _____ care.

2. Although his _____ language is Portuguese, Alberto speaks English fluently.

3. The summit brought together several countries in an attempt to improve _____ relations.

4. Although Rhonda enjoys watching science fiction movies, she does not believe in _____ phenomena.

5. Before becoming a(n) _____ citizen of the United States, a person must have an understanding of U.S. history and government.

12

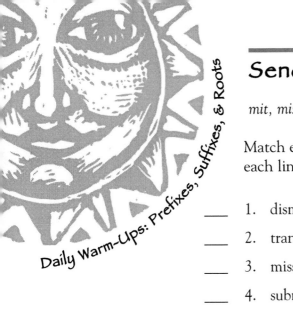

Send Away!

mit, miss—roots meaning *to send*

Match each word to its definition by writing the correct letter on each line.

_____ 1. dismiss

_____ 2. transmit

_____ 3. missile

_____ 4. submit

_____ 5. missive

_____ 6. permit

a. to present for review

b. to allow; to authorize

c. a weapon that is thrown

d. written communication; letter

e. to allow to leave

f. to send

13

© 2006 Walch Publishing

What Does It Mean? I

Choose the correct word from the box below to complete each sentence. Then answer the question that follows.

scribble   nondescript   inscription   transcribe   postscript

1. There isn't much to say about the town we visited; it was very dull and _____.

2. The job of the court reporter is to _____ everything that was said so that there is a written record.

3. The _____ on the pocket watch indicated that it was from 1853.

4. At the end of her e-mail, Jennie added a(n) _____.

5. My little brother doesn't know how to write yet, but he likes to _____ on a sheet of paper.

14

6. Using the context clues in the sentences above, what do you think the roots *scrib* and *script* mean?

More Number Roots

The following roots have number meanings:

mono, uni—one   *tetra, quadr*—four

di, bi, du—two   *penta*—five

tri—three

Match each word to its definition by writing the correct letter on each line.

___ 1. united   a. occurring every two years

___ 2. biennial   b. four-legged creature

___ 3. triathlon   c. star with five points

___ 4. quadruped   d. brought together as one

___ 5. pentagram   e. athletic competition with three events

15

Even More Number Roots

The following roots have number meanings:

quint—five

hex—six

sept, hept—seven

oct—eight

nove—nine

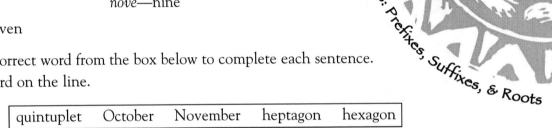

Choose the correct word from the box below to complete each sentence. Write the word on the line.

| quintuplet | October | November | heptagon | hexagon |

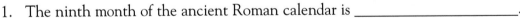

1. The ninth month of the ancient Roman calendar is _____.

2. A(n) _____ is a shape with seven angles.

3. One of five children born at the same time is a(n) _____.

4. _____ used to be the eighth month in the calendar in ancient Roman times.

5. A six-sided shape is called a(n) _____.

16

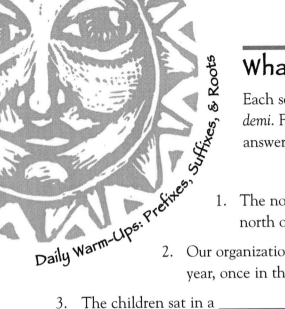

What Does It Mean? II

Each sentence is missing one of the following roots: *semi*, *hemi*, or *demi*. Fill in the missing root to complete each sentence. Then answer the question that follows.

1. The northern _____ sphere is the half of the earth that is north of the equator.

2. Our organization's _____ annual fund-raiser takes place every half-year, once in the fall and once in the spring.

3. The children sat in a _____ circle around their teacher while he read them a story.

4. A _____ god is a mythological creature that is half-man and half-god.

5. What do *semi*, *hemi*, and *demi* mean? _____

17

Don't Ask!

quer, ques, quir, quis—roots meaning *to ask*

Match each word to its definition by writing the correct letter on each line.

___ 1. Somebody who is very curious is _____.

___ 2. A(n) _____ is the same thing as a question.

___ 3. To _____ means to ask for or to demand.

___ 4. A(n) _____ is a search, often involving a journey or an adventure.

___ 5. Something that is asked is a(n) _____.

a. require

b. inquisitive

c. query

d. quest

e. question

18

War and Peace

pac—root meaning *peace*

bell, belli—root meaning *war*

Choose the correct word to complete each sentence.

1. The artifact dated back to before the Civil War; it was from the _____ period.

   a. antebellum   b. pacific

2. The crying child would not be _____ until his favorite toy was found.

   a. bellicose   b. pacified

3. While many people think of chimpanzees as peaceful creatures, they can actually be quite _____.

   a. belligerent   b. pacifying

19

What Does It Mean? III

Complete the following sentences by filling in the missing root.
Then answer the questions that follow.

1. A caterpillar undergoes a meta_____osis before emerging as a butterfly.

2. While clouds appear to be a_____ous at first, if you look at them for a while, they begin to appear to have distinct shapes.

3. In mythology, some gods are anthropo_____ic, meaning that they take the shape of a person.

4. What is the missing root? _____

5. What do you think it means? _____

20

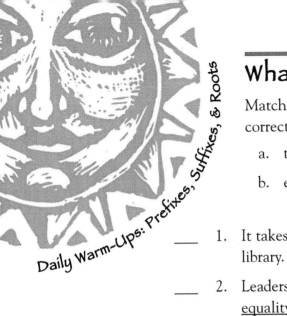

What Does It Mean? IV

Match each underlined word to its definition by writing the correct letter on the line. Then answer the question that follows.

a. to treat as comparable

b. equal in amount

c. equal treatment

d. same distance

____ 1. It takes me the same amount of time to get to the park or the library. The park and the library are <u>equidistant</u> from my house.

____ 2. Leaders of the American civil rights movement worked to gain <u>equality</u> for all people.

____ 3. One cup of the concentrated cleaner is the <u>equivalent</u> of three cups of regular cleaner.

____ 4. It is impossible to <u>equate</u> my experience to yours. They are completely different.

5. What does the root *equ* mean?

a. even, same   b. opposite, different   c. speak, say

21

Small or Large?

macro—root meaning *large*

min—root meaning *small*

Match each word to its definition by writing the correct letter on each line.

_____ 1. macrocosm

_____ 2. minimum

_____ 3. diminutive

_____ 4. macroscopic

_____ 5. microscopic

a. universe

b. too small to be seen with the naked eye

c. large enough to be seen with the naked eye

d. smallest amount

e. tiny

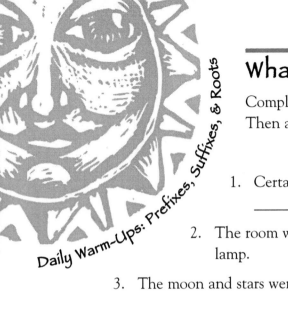

What's Missing? 1

Complete the following sentences by filling in the missing root. Then answer the questions that follow.

1. Certain living creatures, such as fireflies, have a quality called _____inescence, which means that they glow.

2. The room was dark until I il_____inated it by switching on a lamp.

3. The moon and stars were _____inous in the night sky.

4. What is the missing root? _____

5. What do you think it means? _____

23

Daily Warm-Ups: Prefixes, Suffixes, & Roots

Common Root 1

Choose the correct word from the box below to complete each sentence. Write the word on the line. Then answer the questions that follow.

| collaborate | laboratory | elaborate | labor |

1. The team hatched a(n) _____ plan to steal their rival's mascot.

2. Instead of working individually, we'll form groups and _____ on our projects.

3. The scientist spent long hours in her _____ studying different types of bacteria.

4. Painting the house was a long, _____ -intensive process, but the end result was worth it.

5. What is the common root in all the words in the box? _____

6. What does the root most likely mean? _____

24

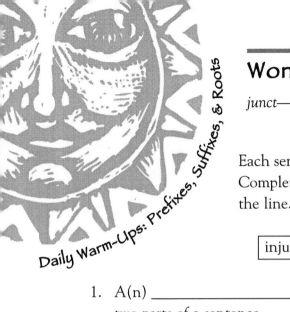

Won't You Join Us?

junct—root meaning *to join*

Each sentence is missing a word that contains the root *junct*. Complete each sentence by writing a word from the box on the line.

injunction	juncture	junction	conjunction

1. A(n) _____ is a word, such as *and* or *but*, that connects two parts of a sentence.

2. About a mile down the road, there is a(n) _____ where two roads come together.

3. It was a fateful _____ in time when the two heads of state met with each other.

4. A(n) _____ is a court order.

25

I Can't Hear You!

aud—root meaning *to hear*

Each of these sentences is missing a common word that contains the
root *aud*. Complete each sentence by writing the word on the line.

1. Having performed mostly on television, the actor was not used to
   working in front of a live _____.

2. The singer's voice was barely _____ above the loud
   music.

3. The popular speaker packed the _____ ; not a single seat
   was left empty.

4. After her _____, Therese waited to hear if she got the
   part in the play.

5. The teacher used _____ materials, which combined
   both sound and sight, to teach the lesson.

26

What Does It Mean? V

Read the sentences below. Then answer the questions that follow.

Someone who is **omniscient** knows everything.

Something that is **omnipresent** is present everywhere.

Someone who is **omnipotent** has complete power.

An **omnivore** is a person or animal that eats everything.

1. Based on the clues in the sentences above, what do you think the root *omni* means?

   a. few   c. power

   b. all   d. knowledge

2. Now write a sentence of your own containing a word with the root *omni*.

27

What's Missing? II

Complete the following sentences by filling in the missing root.
Then answer the questions that follow.

28

1. Although driving a car is a convenient form of
   trans_____ation, alternatives include walking, bicycling,
   and taking the bus.

2. The ship carried goods that were being im_____ed to the United
   States from Spain.

3. The room was chilly, so I turned on the _____able heater.

4. Before they were taken to a restaurant, the children were warned to
   com_____ themselves properly.

5. What is the missing root? _____

6. What does it mean?

   a. walk   b. carry   c. try

Daily Warm-Ups: Prefixes, Suffixes, & Roots

Don't Touch!

tact—root meaning *touch*

Match each underlined word to its definition. Write the letter of the definition on the line.

    a. delicate, sensitive in dealing with others

    b. untouched, unharmed

    c. touching, coming together

    d. relating to the sense of touch

____ 1. Kneading dough is a <u>tactile</u> experience.

____ 2. The passengers cheered when the wheels of the airplane made <u>contact</u> with the runway.

____ 3. Somehow, the lamp remained <u>intact</u> even after it crashed to the floor.

____ 4. Although Kyla hated her friend's new haircut, she made an effort to be <u>tactful</u> about it.

What's Missing? III

Each of the following sentences is missing a word. All of the words share the same root. Complete each sentence by writing the missing word on the line. Then answer the questions that follow.

1. An instrument that measures heat is called a

   _____.

2. A container designed to keep liquid hot is called a

   _____.

3. In order to turn up the heat in your house, you adjust the

   _____.

4. What is the common root? _____

5. What does the root mean? _____

30

Divide and Conquer

Vinc, *vict*, and *vanq* are all roots that mean *to conquer*.

Complete each sentence below by filling in the missing root.

1. Our team is hoping for a _____ory in the game this Saturday.

2. The warrior fought hard to _____uish his enemy.

3. After winning the game, we felt that our team was in_____ible.

4. After a lengthy trial, the criminal was finally con_____ed.

5. No matter how much I argued, I could not con_____e anyone that I was right.

6. After not paying rent for months, the tenant was e_____ed.

31

What Time Is It?

chron—root meaning *time*

Read each sentence. Use context and the meaning of the root to find the meaning of each underlined word. Then write a definition of each word.

1. The actor's modern watch was <u>anachronistic</u> in a play set in the 1700s.

   anachronistic: _____

2. In history class, we created a <u>chronology</u> of the Civil War.

   chronology: _____

3. Let's <u>synchronize</u> our watches so that we can meet back here at 4 P.M.

   synchronize: _____

4. The paper listed the most important events in <u>chronological</u> order.

   chronological: _____

32

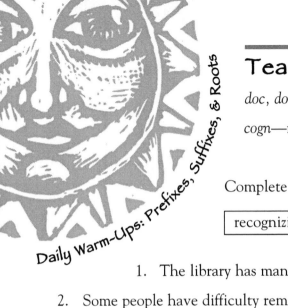

Teaching and Learning

doc, doct—roots meaning *to teach*

cogn—root meaning *to learn*

Complete each sentence with a word from the box.

| recognizing | indoctrination | docile | cognition | documents |

1. The library has many historical _____ in its archive.

2. Some people have difficulty remembering names, while others have trouble _____ faces.

3. Studies of primate _____ shed light on the thought processes of animals.

4. The meeting served as a(n) _____ into the organization's belief system.

5. I thought that my new puppy would be aggressive and difficult to train, but he turned out to be quite _____.

33

Daily Warm-Ups: Prefixes, Suffixes, & Roots

Context Clues

The underlined words in the following sentences all contain the root *nov*. Read each sentence, and use the context clues to write the meaning on the line. Then answer the question that follows.

1. She enjoyed each new toy until the <u>novelty</u> wore off and it was no longer interesting to her.

   novelty: _____

2. As a <u>novice</u> skater, Julia falls a lot, but her balance will improve as she gains experience.

   novice: _____

3. The advertising agency wanted to come up with some <u>innovative</u> ideas instead of the same old, stale ones.

   innovative: _____

4. What does the root *nov* mean? _____

34

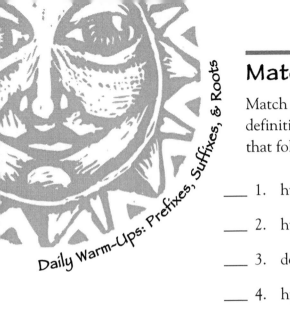

Match It Up!

Match each word to its definition. Write the letter of the definition on the line provided. Then answer the question that follows.

____ 1. hydrated

____ 2. hydrant

____ 3. dehydrate

____ 4. hydraulic

____ 5. hydrosphere

a. operated by water

b. to remove water

c. water vapor in the atmosphere

d. given water

e. discharge pipe for water main; fireplug

6. What does the root *hydra* mean? _____

35

To Have and to Hold

ten, tain—roots meaning *to hold*

Choose the correct word to complete each sentence. Circle the letter of the correct answer.

1. After the large meal, we were _____ just to sit back in our chairs and relax.

   a. content   b. contentious   c. detained

2. At the beginning of our hike we walked very quickly, but we were unable to _____ that pace for very long.

   a. pertain   b. sustain   c. detain

3. It is unlikely that you will _____ great wealth by winning the lottery.

   a. contain   b. entertain   c. obtain

4. Part of my job is to repair and _____ the machines.

   a. detain   b. maintain   c. abstain

Daily Warm-Ups: Prefixes, Suffixes, & Roots

36

Common Root II

The underlined words in the following sentences all contain a common root. Read each sentence. Then use the context clues to answer the questions that follow.

Although the human population keeps growing, the supply of drinkable water is <u>finite</u>.

After we <u>finish</u> priming the walls, we'll be ready to paint the room.

The fireworks display was impressive from the beginning, but the <u>finale</u> was truly spectacular.

With so many different activities to choose from, the options seemed almost <u>infinite</u>.

1. What is the common root in the underlined words? _____

2. What do you think the root means? _____

37

More Body Parts

Read the definitions below. Then answer the questions that follow.

dermatologist—a doctor who treats skin

epidermis—the outer layer of the skin

hemoglobin—a pigment in red blood cells that helps transport oxygen

hemophilia—a rare condition in which blood does not clot properly

ossification—the process of changing into bone

osteoplasty—surgery that corrects problems with bones

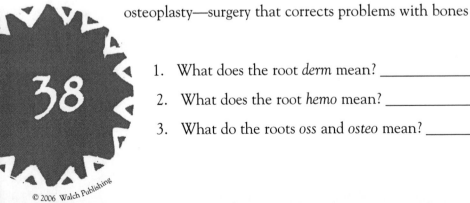

38

1. What does the root *derm* mean? _____

2. What does the root *hemo* mean? _____

3. What do the roots *oss* and *osteo* mean? _____

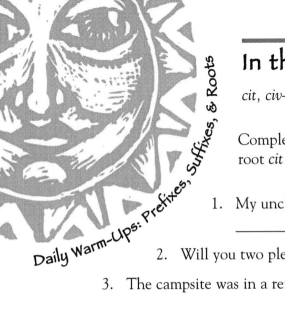

Daily Warm-Ups: Prefixes, Suffixes, & Roots

In the City

cit, civ—roots meaning *city*

Complete each sentence with a common word that contains the root *cit* or *civ*. Write the word on the line.

1. My uncle just moved here from Italy. He is not a U.S. _____.

2. Will you two please stop fighting and just be _____?

3. The campsite was in a remote part of the woods, far from _____.

4. Many people consider voting to be their _____ duty.

5. A person who is not part of the military is called a _____.

39

© 2006 Walch Publishing

Plants and Animals

botan—root meaning *plant*

zoo—root meaning *animal*

Complete each sentence with a word from the box. Write the correct word on the line.

botany	zoology	botanist	zoologist	zoo	botanical

40

1. A person who studies animals is a _____.

2. The study of plants is called _____.

3. The study of animals is called _____.

4. A person who wished to see animals would visit a _____.

5. A _____ society would be dedicated to the preservation of plants.

6. A _____ is a person who studies plants.

Highs and Lows

bas—root meaning *low*

alt—root meaning *high*

Complete each sentence with a common word using the root *bas* or *alt*. Write the word on the line. Use the clues in parentheses to help.

1. The part of a house that is below the ground is called the (sublevel) _____.

2. After takeoff, the airplane gained _____ (height) until it was 10,000 feet above the ground.

3. It is important to learn the _____ (fundamentals) of skiing before trying any complicated moves.

4. The citizens applauded enthusiastically for their _____ (high-ranking) leader.

5. Our band has a drummer and a lead guitar, but we really need someone to play _____ (low in pitch) guitar.

41

I Don't Care!

cur—root meaning *care*

Match each word to its definition. Write the letter of the definition on the line.

42

___ 1. curator

___ 2. curative

___ 3. curable

___ 4. secure

___ 5. sinecure

a. something used to cure diseases

b. paid job that requires little work to be done

c. safe

d. able to be made better

e. person in charge of something, such as a museum

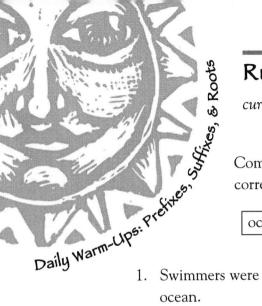

Run!

cur, curr, curs—roots meaning *to run*

Complete each sentence with a word from the box. Write the correct word on the line.

occur	excursion	current	cursory	precursor

1. Swimmers were warned to be careful of the strong _____ in the ocean.

2. After staying in all week, we were ready for a(n) _____ downtown.

3. The telegraph was the _____ to the modern-day telephone.

4. After a(n) _____ glance at his textbook, Roy announced that he was finished studying.

5. Traffic accidents used to _____ regularly at the intersection until the city installed a traffic light.

43

© 2006 Walch Publishing

Night and Day

noct—root meaning *night*

journ—root meaning *day*

Complete each sentence with a common word that contains either the root *noct* or the root *journ*. Write the word on the line. Use the clues in parentheses to help you.

1. A _____ (diary) is a daily record of a person's thoughts.

2. The first leg of the _____ (long trip) is an airplane flight; after that, we'll get on a train and then, finally, a bus.

3. Owls are _____ (active at night) creatures that are well adapted to the dark.

4. The judge decreed that court would _____ (be suspended until another time) until the following day.

Stretch

ten, tend, tens—roots meaning *to stretch*

Read each sentence. Use the meaning of the root and the context of the sentence to help you figure out the meaning of each underlined word. Then write a definition of each word on the line.

1. The dancer balanced on one foot and <u>extended</u> her other leg.

   extended: _____

2. Another person might have given up the search, but Tanya was very <u>tenacious</u> and refused to abandon her effort.

   tenacious: _____

3. The rope must not sag; pull it so that there is <u>tension</u> in the middle.

   tension: _____

4. He has a <u>tendency</u> to agree with whatever anyone says at the time.

   tendency: _____

45

Not Too Swift

celer—root meaning *fast*

Read each sentence. Use the meaning of the root and the context of the sentence to help you figure out the meaning of each underlined word. Then write a definition of each word on the line.

1. The car can <u>accelerate</u> quickly, reaching a high speed in a very short amount of time.

   accelerate: _____

2. The cheetah is known for its <u>celerity</u>; it is the fastest animal on land.

   celerity: _____

3. Once the cart reaches the bottom of the hill, it will begin to <u>decelerate</u> until it rolls to a stop.

   decelerate: _____

46

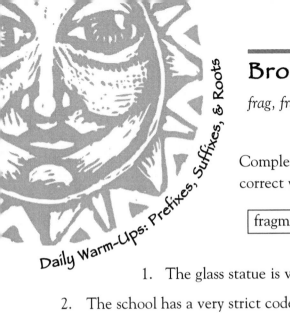

Broken

frag, fract—roots meaning *to break*

Complete each sentence with a word from the box. Write the correct word on the line.

fragment	fracture	fragile	infraction	fraction

1. The glass statue is very _____; it could easily be broken.

2. The school has a very strict code of conduct, and even the slightest _____ is grounds for punishment.

3. Fortunately, Sarah's injury from the fall was very minor. She received only a small _____ that will heal easily.

4. The archeologist discovered a _____ of pottery that she believed to be hundreds of years old.

5. The teacher spends only a _____ of his time in the classroom; he spends the rest of his day grading papers and preparing lessons.

47

© 2006 Walch Publishing

Daily Warm-Ups: Prefixes, Suffixes, & Roots

Deceit

fall, fals—roots meaning *to deceive*

Read each sentence. Then choose the definition for the underlined word by circling the correct letter.

1. The statement was a <u>fallacy</u>; it was based on untrue assumptions.

    a. true statement   b. false or mistaken idea   c. prediction of the future

2. Miranda was accused of <u>falsifying</u> her time sheets for work, but she was able to prove that they were accurate.

    a. making untrue   b. creating from scratch   c. double-checking

3. Jake insisted that his memory was <u>infallible</u>, but there were many recent events that he could not recall.

    a. deliberately incorrect   b. somewhat hazy   c. incapable of error

4. The defendant told a <u>fallacious</u> story in the hope it would hide his guilt.

    a. honest   b. misleading   c. accurate

48

Daily Warm-Ups: Prefixes, Suffixes, & Roots

Definition, Please!

Read each sentence. Use the meaning of the root and the context of the sentence to help you figure out the meaning of each underlined word. Then write a definition of each word on the line. Use these definitions to help you answer question 4.

1. Once <u>liberated</u> from its cage, the parrot flew straight to the windowsill.

   liberated: _____

2. The students were at <u>liberty</u> to spend their free time however they chose.

   liberty: _____

3. The wealthy donor gave <u>liberally</u> to many worthy causes.

   liberally: _____

4. What does the root *liber* mean? _____

49

To Change or Not to Change?

mut—root meaning *change*

Complete each sentence with a word from the box. Write the correct word on the line.

mutate	immutable	commute	permutation

1. The big disadvantage of living so far from work is the long

   _____.

2. I've figured out every possible _____ of the seating chart for the wedding.

3. A gene can _____, so that there is a permanent change in the genetic material.

4. The landscape seemed _____, but over time, it changed.

50

Not I

in-, im-, ir-, il- — prefixes meaning *not*

Add the correct prefix to complete each sentence. Write the prefix on the line.

1. It was _____responsible of you to drive the car without permission.

2. At first, the idea seemed completely _____sane, but after a while it began to sound more reasonable.

3. Your argument is _____logical; it makes no sense.

4. Typing manuscripts on a manual typewriter, once a common practice, is now considered to be outdated and _____efficient.

5. It will be ____possible to make the trip in less than five hours.

51

Not II

a- —prefix meaning *not*

Write the word that each definition describes on the line. Each
word contains the prefix *a-*.

1. _____: having no morals

2. _____: not typical, unusual

3. _____: not symmetrical

4. _____: lacking tone

5. _____: lacking color

6. Now write a sentence of your own using one of the words above.

52

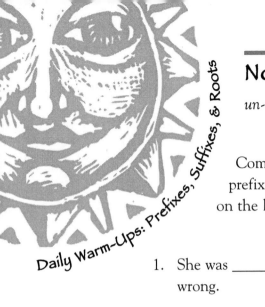

Not III

un- —prefix meaning *not*

Complete each sentence using a common word that contains the prefix *un-*. Use the clues in parentheses to help you. Write the word on the line.

1. She was _____ (not wanting) to admit that she was wrong.

2. We were very _____ (sad) when we heard the bad news.

3. The painting looked like a million other paintings; it was a very _____ (not a new idea) work of art.

4. Because the road's surface was _____ (not smooth), the ride was a bumpy one.

5. Although the staff tried their best, many of the company's goals remained _____ (not reached).

53

© 2006 Walch Publishing

Not IV

dis- —prefix meaning *not*

Match each word to its definition. Write the letter of the definition on the line.

___ 1. disregard   a. differ in opinion

___ 2. disrespect   b. unhappiness

___ 3. discover   c. ignore

___ 4. disagree   d. lack of esteem

___ 5. displeasure   e. find

54

6. Now use one of the words above in a sentence of your own.

Not V

You have learned several different prefixes that mean *not*.
Complete the following sentences by adding the correct prefix
meaning *not*. Write the prefix on the line.

1. She can't decide what to do. She is _____decisive.

2. He has no sympathy for others. He is _____sympathetic.

3. She can barely express an opinion. She is _____articulate.

4. The student has not learned to read. He is _____literate.

5. The glass has no color. It is _____chromatic.

6. The food looked very unappetizing. We looked at it with _____taste.

Daily Warm-Ups: Prefixes, Suffixes, & Roots

Tell Me What It Means!

In the following sentences, each underlined word contains the prefix *anti-*. Read each sentence. Use context clues to help you figure out the meaning of each underlined word. Write a definition of each word on the line. Then answer the question that follows.

1. In order to prevent the spread of infection, many people use <u>antibacterial</u> soap.

   antibacterial: _____

2. He and I disagree about everything. Everything he says is <u>antithetical</u> to my beliefs.

   antithetical: _____

3. I expected to feel a strong sense of <u>antipathy</u> toward my opponent in the election. Instead, I found that I liked her very much.

   antipathy: _____

4. What does the prefix *anti-* mean? _____

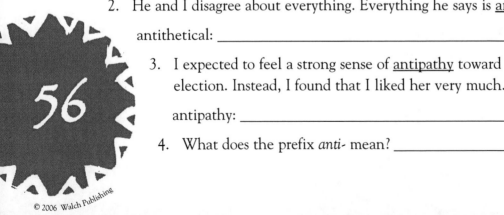

56

Going In!

en-, em- —prefixes meaning *in*

Complete each sentence by writing the correct prefix on the line.

1. The fence _____closes the yard.

2. The rock was so firmly ____bedded in the ground that it was difficult to pull out.

3. He was so _____grossed in his book that he didn't hear the phone ring.

4. Before I realized it, I was _____meshed in an elaborate drama.

5. The brothers, who hadn't seen each other in decades, _____braced warmly.

57

Across the Way

dia- —prefix meaning *across*

Complete each of the following sentences with a word that contains the prefix *dia-*.

1. A chart or drawing that demonstrates how something works is called a
   _____.

2. The distance across a circle is its _____.

3. A line that cuts a rectangle into two triangles is a _____ line.

4. A conversation between two or more people is called a _____.

5. To recognize a disease based on its symptoms is to _____ it.

58

Daily Warm-Ups: Prefixes, Suffixes, & Roots

Over and Under

over- —prefix meaning *too much*

under- —prefix meaning *too little*

Write a definition for each word on the line.

1. overpriced: _____

2. overrated: _____

3. overstated: _____

4. underappreciated: _____

5. underestimated: _____

6. undercooked: _____

59

Hyper and Hypo

Read each sentence. Circle the letter of the correct definition for each underlined word. Then answer the questions that follow.

1. Jack's description of his busy day was largely <u>hyperbole</u>; in fact, very little had actually happened to him.

    a. accurate description   b. exaggeration   c. thoughtful interpretation

2. The child could not sit still for more than a second; she was <u>hyperactive</u>.

    a. overly active   b. quiet   c. too talkative

3. Divers wear insulated suits to prevent <u>hypothermia</u> when they are in cold water.

    a. extra oxygen   b. low body temperature   c. lack of energy

4. If Abby does not eat frequent snacks to keep her blood sugar high enough, she gets <u>hypoglycemic</u>.

    a. good appetite   b. lacking enthusiasm   c. having low blood sugar

5. What does the prefix *hyper* mean? _____

6. What does the prefix *hypo* mean? _____

Match Away!

Read each sentence below, paying particular attention to the underlined words. Then match each prefix to its meaning. Use the context clues in the sentences to help you. Write the letter of the meaning on the line.

The <u>intraoffice</u> memo informed everyone in the office of the upcoming blood drive.

We drove on the <u>interstate</u> because it was the fastest connection between the two states.

The best way to get around the city is by <u>subway</u>, which runs underground.

A <u>supersonic</u> airplane travels faster than the speed of sound.

____ 1. intra   a. below

____ 2. inter   b. above

____ 3. sub   c. between

____ 4. super   d. within

61

Daily Warm-Ups: Prefixes, Suffixes, & Roots

Before, After, and Again

pre- —prefix meaning *before*

post- —prefix meaning *after*

re- —prefix meaning *again*

Complete each sentence by writing in the prefix *pre-*, *post-*, *or re-*.

1. The _____amble to the Constitution of the United States is the document's introduction.

2. Because I didn't understand the chapter, I'll have to _____read it.

3. The new mother recovered from childbirth in the _____natal ward.

4. The carnival fortune-teller claimed that she could _____dict the future.

5. After taking an initial look at the proposal, the committee will _____view it and then vote.

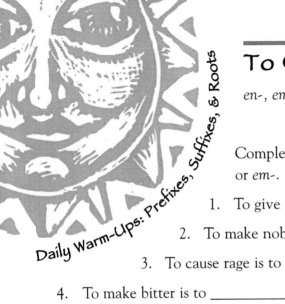

To Cause to Be

en-, em- —prefixes meaning *to cause to be*

Complete each sentence with a word that contains the prefix *en-* or *em-*.

1. To give power is to _____.

2. To make noble is to _____.

3. To cause rage is to _____.

4. To make bitter is to _____.

5. To make large is to _____.

6. Think of other words that contain the prefixes *en-* or *em-*. List as many of them as you can.

63

Put Me In!

in-, im- —prefixes meaning *in* or *into*

Complete each sentence by filling in the correct word from the box.
Write the word on the line.

impress	inhale	immerse	induce

1. Some people believe that the best way to learn a foreign language is to
   _____ oneself in it completely.

2. Despite her efforts, Kaitlyn was unable to _____ her friend
   to run for the position of class president.

3. The teacher tried to _____ upon his students the
   importance of good study habits.

4. Every person who walked into the bakery paused to
   _____ the smell of baking bread.

64

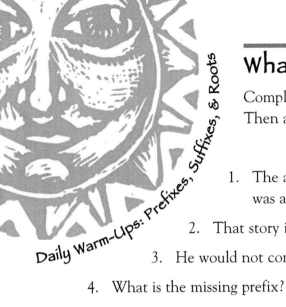

What's the Missing Prefix?

Complete the following sentences by filling in the missing prefix. Then answer the questions that follow.

1. The article gave a factual account of a historic event. The article was a work of _____fiction.

2. That story is utter _____sense; it could not possibly have happened.

3. He would not commit to any particular plan; he was _____committal.

4. What is the missing prefix? _____

5. What is the meaning of the missing prefix? _____

65

You Must Be Mistaken!

The underlined words in the following sentences all contain a common prefix. Read each sentence. Then use the context clues to answer the question that follows.

I thought I saw you at the concert, but I might have been <u>mistaken</u>.

If the children <u>misbehave</u>, they won't go to the movies today.

You're wearing <u>mismatched</u> socks; one is blue and the other is brown.

The animals at the shelter receive a lot of attention and kindness; they are never <u>mistreated</u>.

66

What does the prefix *mis-* mean?

a. over

b. small

c. bad

Daily Warm-Ups: Prefixes, Suffixes, & Roots

A Prefix

Complete each sentence with a word from the box. Write the correct word on the line provided. Then answer the question that follows by circling the letter of the correct answer.

ashore	afoot	affix	aboard

1. Before you mail the letter, be sure to _____ a stamp to it.

2. We climbed _____ the train just before it pulled out of the station.

3. Walking along the beach, you'll find that many interesting things wash _____.

4. The dog watched suspiciously as his owners set out his traveling crate; he knew that something was _____.

5. What does the prefix *a-* mean, as it is used in the words above?

   a. from   b. on   c. too many

67

© 2006 Walch Publishing

Extra, Extra!

extra-, extro- —prefix meaning *beyond, outside*

Complete each sentence with a word that begins with the prefix
extra- or *extro-*. Write the word on the line.

1. A being from beyond Earth is an _____.

2. Activities that are outside of the regular school curriculum are

    _____.

3. Something that is out of the ordinary is _____.

4. Somebody with an outgoing personality is called an

    _____.

5. Something that costs more than is reasonable is _____.

68

All Aboard!

pan- —prefix meaning *all*

Match each underlined word to its definition below. Write the letter of the definition on the line.

a. tumult, uproar

b. occurring over a wide area

c. view in every direction

d. cure-all

___ 1. If a remedy is marketed as a <u>panacea</u>, it is almost certainly a fake.

___ 2. From the top of the mountain, we enjoyed a magnificent <u>panorama</u>.

___ 3. The classroom was noisy and chaotic; the scene was one of <u>pandemonium</u>.

___ 4. Health officials worked hard to prevent the illness from becoming <u>pandemic</u>.

69

Meta Match

Match each word to its definition. Write the letter of the definition on the line. Then answer the question that follows.

___ 1. metaphor

___ 2. metamorphosis

___ 3. metabolism

a. chemical changes in cells that turn fuel into energy

b. figure of speech in which one phrase is exchanged for another to indicate similarity

c. change in physical form

4. What does the prefix *meta-* mean? _____

70

How Many?

mono- —prefix meaning *one*

multi- —prefix meaning *many*

olig- —prefix meaning *few*

Complete each sentence by writing the correct prefix on the line.

1. A(n) _____archy is a government in which a few people rule.

2. The meeting was painfully _____tonous; it seemed as though each speaker said the same thing as the last.

3. The peace accord was not between just two countries; it was a _____lateral agreement that involved the entire region.

4. Unlike a train, which runs on a track made of two rails, a _____rail runs on a single rail.

5. He tried _____ple times to reach his brother by phone, but he wouldn't answer.

71

Going Through

per- —prefix meaning *through, across*

Read each sentence. Use the meaning of *per-* and the context clues to help you figure out the meaning of each underlined word. Write a definition of each word on the line.

1. The smell of the baking cake <u>pervaded</u> the air.

    pervaded: _____

2. I had hoped that my umbrella was <u>impermeable</u>, but then I noticed a leak.

    impermeable: _____

3. Each candidate tried to <u>persuade</u> the audience that he or she was the best person for the job.

    persuade: _____

4. I was worried about finding information for my research paper, but I discovered that the library contains several books <u>pertaining</u> to my topic.

    pertaining: _____

72

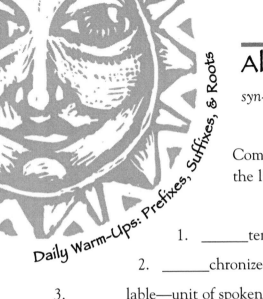

All Together

syn-, sym-, syl-, sys- —prefixes meaning *with, together*

Complete the defined words by writing the correct prefix on the line.

1. _____tem—different pieces working together to form a unit

2. _____chronize—set to the same time

3. _____lable—unit of spoken language

4. _____pathy—similarity in action or feeling

5. _____tax—the way words are put together; grammar

6. _____bol—something that represents something else

73

Far Away

tele- —prefix meaning *distant, far*

Match each word to its definition. Write the letter of the correct definition on the line.

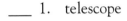

_____ 1. telescope

_____ 2. telegraph

_____ 3. telemeter

_____ 4. telephone

a. device that takes measurements at a distance

b. device that allows a person to speak over long distances

c. device that electronically transmits signals over a wire

d. instrument used to view distant objects

74

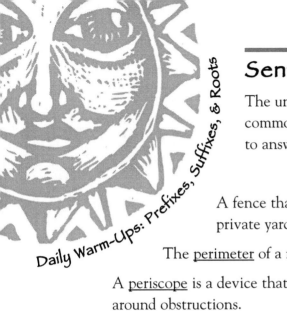

Sentence Clues

The underlined words in the following sentences all contain a common prefix. Read each sentence. Then use the context clues to answer the question that follows.

A fence that ran along the park's <u>periphery</u> separated the park from a private yard.

The <u>perimeter</u> of a rectangle is the lengths of all the sides, added together.

A <u>periscope</u> is a device that uses lenses and mirrors so that a person can see around obstructions.

What does the prefix *peri-* mean?

a. after

b. beneath

c. around

75

That's a Fake!

pseudo- —prefix meaning *false*

Read each sentence. Use the meaning of *pseudo-* and the context clues to help you figure out the meaning of each underlined word. Write a definition of each word on the line.

1. George Eliot was not the author's real name; it was a <u>pseudonym</u>.

   pseudonym: _____

2. The study was poorly conducted and logically flawed. It was not real science; it was <u>pseudoscience</u>.

   pseudoscience: _____

3. The sculpture had some of the elements of classic design, but it was not truly classic in style. It was <u>pseudoclassic</u>.

   pseudoclassic: _____

76

Daily Warm-Ups: Prefixes, Suffixes, & Roots

Close Prefixes

The underlined words in the following sentences all contain a common prefix. Read each sentence. Then use the context clues to answer the question that follows.

A <u>polygamist</u> is a person who has several spouses.

A <u>polygon</u> is a shape with many sides.

A <u>polysyllabic</u> word has many syllables.

Which prefix is *poly-* closest to in meaning?

   a. *multi-*

   b. *bi-*

   c. *mono-*

77

Go Away!

se- —prefix meaning *away, apart*

Complete each sentence with a word from the box. Write the correct word on the line provided.

secession	seclusion	separate	segregate	secede

1. Each group took the test in a _____ room.

2. After several days of _____, Jacob looked forward to being around people again.

3. Some of the state's residents wanted it to withdraw from the Union, but other residents thought that _____ was a bad idea.

4. Because disease can spread quickly, it is important to _____ sick animals and keep them away from healthy ones.

5. The island community voted to _____ from the town and become independent.

78

Are We Related?

para- —prefix meaning *alongside, related*

Complete each sentence with a common word that begins with the prefix *para-*.

1. A rectangle has two pairs of _____ sides.

2. A device used to slow a person's fall from an airplane is called a _____.

3. To put something into your own words is to _____.

4. A statement that seems to contradict itself is a _____.

5. A group of sentences organized around one topic is a _____.

79

Where Are You From?

ab- —prefix meaning *from*, *away from*

Complete each sentence with a word from the box. Write the correct word on the line.

| absent | abstract | abstain | abscond | abhor |

1. The thieves planned to _____ with the jewels.

2. I don't love green beans, but I don't _____ them, either.

3. Jessie was _____ from school because she was sick.

4. The painting, a swirl of colors, was an _____ representation of the town.

5. We decided to _____ from dessert, since we'd had such a large dinner.

80

Not a Review

Write the correct prefix on the line to give each word its opposite meaning.

1. The movie was filled with so many coincidences that the plot seemed _____believable.

2. The broken vase was one of a kind; it was _____replaceable.

3. Sam doesn't like to behave like everybody else; she is a _____conformist.

4. Please _____regard the earlier memo; it was incorrect.

5. The pile of dead leaves began to _____compose.

81

Come Toward Me

ad- —prefix meaning *to, toward*

Complete each sentence with a word from the box. Write the correct word on the line.

adorn	advert	adjacent	admit	adventure

1. To venture forth is to have an _____.

2. To call attention to something is to _____ to it.

3. To let a person into a club is to _____ him or her.

4. To decorate something with ornaments is to _____ it.

5. Two towns that are next to each other are _____.

82

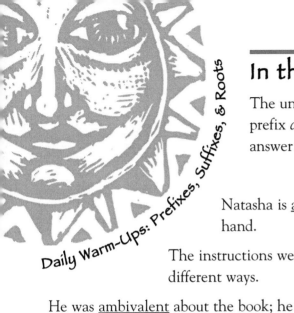

Daily Warm-Ups: Prefixes, Suffixes, & Roots

In the Context

The underlined words in the following sentences all contain the prefix *ambi-*. Read each sentence. Then use the context clues to answer the question that follows.

Natasha is <u>ambidextrous</u>; she can write with either her right or left hand.

The instructions were very <u>ambiguous</u>; they could be interpreted in two different ways.

He was <u>ambivalent</u> about the book; he liked it, and yet he didn't like it.

What does the prefix *ambi-* mean?

   a. neither

   b. both

   c. without

83

Going Forward

pro- —prefix meaning *forward*

Match each word to its definition. Write the letter of the correct definition on the line.

_____ 1. propel

_____ 2. produce

_____ 3. proactive

_____ 4. proceed

_____ 5. promote

a. to bring about, to create

b. foreseeing and preparing for problems ahead of time

c. to drive forward; to physically cause something to move

d. to move forward with something

e. to publicize; to advance to higher rank

It's in the Definition!

Read the following definitions. Then answer the question that follows.

protoplasm—the matter that makes up all plant and animal cells

protoplast—a being that is the first of its kind

prototype—something that is the first of its kind

protohistory—the study of humans in the period immediately before recorded history

protohuman—an early human

What does the prefix *proto-* mean?

a. first

b. natural

c. not

85

Daily Warm-Ups: Prefixes, Suffixes, & Roots

Take My Place

vice- —prefix meaning *in place of*

Complete each sentence with a word that contains the prefix *vice*.
Write the word on the line.

Daily Warm-Ups: Prefixes, Suffixes, & Roots

1. The person who is in charge during the president's absence is the

    _____.

2. The person who is in charge during the principal's absence is the

    _____.

3. A naval officer who ranks below an admiral is a _____.

4. A deputy chairman is a _____.

86

With or Without You

with- —prefix meaning *away*, *back* or *against*, *from*

Match each word to its definition. Write the letter of the correct definition on the line.

___ 1. withhold   a. on the interior

___ 2. withstand   b. to take back or remove

___ 3. withdraw   c. to hold back or refrain from granting

___ 4. without   d. on the outside

___ 5. within   e. to resist or endure

87

That's Bad!

dys- —prefix meaning *bad, abnormal*

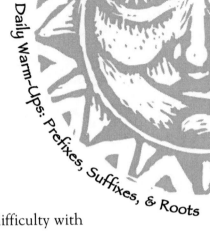

Complete each sentence with a word from the box. Write the correct word on the line.

| dyslexia | dysfunction | dyspepsia | dystopia | dysphonia |

1. _____ is a learning disability involving difficulty with reading and processing language.

2. Another word for indigestion is _____.

3. Lack of normal functioning is _____.

4. A utopia is an ideal world; the opposite of a utopia is a _____.

5. An impairment of the voice is _____.

88

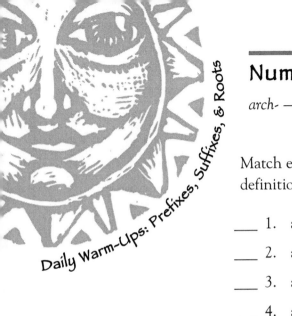

Number One

arch- —prefix meaning *first, chief*

Match each word to its definition. Write the letter of the correct definition on the line.

___ 1. archaic   a. original pattern

___ 2. archenemy   b. belonging to an earlier time period

___ 3. archetype   c. chief foe

___ 4. architect   d. designer

5. Now use one of the words defined above in a sentence of your own.

89

Circle the Meaning

Read the following definitions. Then answer the question that follows.

ultrasonic—frequency of vibrations above the range that can be heard

ultramodern—extremely modern

ultraconservative—very conservative

What does the prefix *ultra-* mean?

    a. excessive, beyond

    b. again, repeated

    c. against, opposite

90

Matching Sentences

contra- —prefix meaning *against, opposite*

Match each underlined word to its definition. Write the letter of the definition on the line.

a. in opposition

b. to show differences

c. to go against, oppose

d. a statement that is opposite to another one

___ 1. The meteorologist's prediction of rain was a <u>contradiction</u> of her earlier statement that it would be sunny all day.

___ 2. Many of his beliefs were <u>contrary</u> to those of his parents.

___ 3. My research paper will <u>contrast</u> pre-Civil War America and post-Civil War America.

___ 4. Because her actions <u>contravene</u> the company's professional code of conduct, she will be put on probation.

91

© 2006 Walch Publishing

Take Me away from Here!

de- —prefix meaning *away from, off*

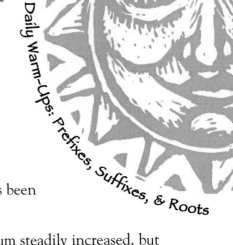

Complete each sentence by changing the underlined word to one
that uses the prefix *de-*. Write the new word on the line.

1. The summer camp used to <u>emphasize</u> sports, but lately it has been
_____ them in favor of the arts.

2. For several years, the number of visitors to the museum steadily <u>increased</u>, but
last year the number _____.

3. We spent an hour <u>inflating</u> our raft, only to have to
_____ it because it wouldn't fit in the car.

4. The lake, once heavily <u>contaminated</u>, has finally been
_____ and can be used for recreation.

5. After <u>accelerating</u> the car for several minutes, the driver began
_____ when the road became curvy.

92

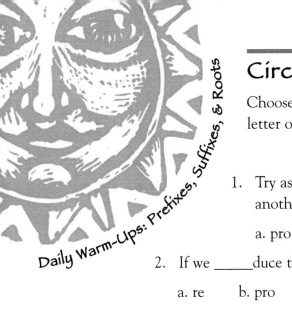

Circle the Prefix 1

Choose the correct prefix to complete each sentence. Circle the letter of the correct answer.

1. Try as we might, we could not _____duce the band to perform another encore.

   a. pro b. re c. in

2. If we _____duce the amount of electricity we use, we will save money.

   a. re b. pro c. de

3. Unless you can _____duce some evidence, no one will believe that story.

   a. in b. pro c. re

4. Based on the clues, I can _____duce that the suspect is in this room.

   a. de b. in c. re

5. The root *duc* means _____.

   a. water b. to silence c. to lead

93

Daily Warm-Ups: Prefixes, Suffixes, & Roots

Circle the Prefix II

Use your knowledge of prefixes to complete each sentence. Circle the letter of the correct answer.

1. A vehicle with one wheel is a _____.

   a. bicycle   b. unicycle   c. tricycle

2. Something that is not accurate is _____accurate.

   a. in   b. dis   c. anti

3. The yard is _____closed by a fence.

   a. in   b. on   c. en

4. The layer of soil beneath the surface is called _____.

   a. supersoil   b. pansoil   c. subsoil

5. Something on the outside is _____.

   a. external   b. internal   c. eternal

94

Prefix Fill-in

Use your knowledge of prefixes to complete the following sentences. Write the correct prefix on the line.

1. Two figures that are not of the same size and shape are _____symmetrical.

2. A person in favor of voting is _____-voting.

3. An instrument that allows the user to see objects that are very far away is a _____scope.

4. To put something off until later is to _____pone it.

5. To make something appear to be larger is to _____fy it.

95

Circle the Prefix III

Use your knowledge of prefixes to answer the following questions.
Circle the letter of the correct answer.

1. How many feet does a quadruped have?

    a. one   b. two   c. four

2. How many feet does a tripod have?

    a. one   b. three   c. five

3. How many times a year does a biannual event occur?

    a. one   b. two   c. five

4. How many years are in a decade?

    a. five   b. ten   c. one hundred

5. A centennial celebrates a _____ anniversary.

    a. tenth   b. fiftieth   c. one hundredth

96

Circle the Prefix IV

Use your knowledge of prefixes to complete the following sentences. Circle the letter of the correct answer.

1. Two things that are poorly matched are ____matched.

   a. dis   b. anti   c. mis

2. Somebody who is not active is ____active.

   a. non   b. in   c. dis

3. People who are not in agreement ____agree.

   a. mal   b. un   c. dis

4. Somebody who is not sane is ____sane.

   a. un   b. in   c. non

5. Somebody who is not comfortable feels ____comfort.

   a. dis   b. mis   c. un

97

© 2006 Walch Publishing

Matching Prefixes 1

Use your knowledge of prefixes to match each word to its definition. Write the letter of the definition on the line provided.

___ 1. predict   a. to come before

___ 2. contradict   b. to speak against

___ 3. precede   c. to say what will happen before it does

___ 4. proceed   d. to move ahead

5. Now use one of the words defined above in a sentence of your own.

98

Matching Prefixes II

Match the prefixes that are similar in meaning. Write the letter of the correct prefix on the line.

____ 1. mono   a. anti

____ 2. poly   b. non

____ 3. un   c. multi

____ 4. contra   d. uni

____ 5. sub   e. under

6. Now think of some words that begin with these prefixes. List as many as you can.

99

Matching Prefixes III

Match the prefixes that are *opposite* in meaning. Write the letter of the correct prefix on the line.

___ 1. bene   a. sub

___ 2. pro   b. mal

___ 3. super   c. pre

___ 4. post   d. anti

___ 5. micro   e. macro

100

6. Now think of some words that begin with these prefixes. List as many as you can.

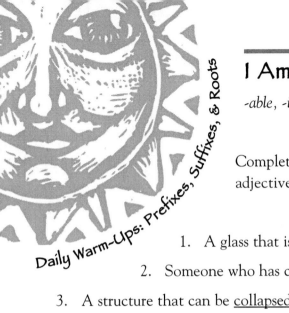

I Am Able

-able, -ible—suffixes meaning *is able*

Complete each sentence by changing the underlined word to an adjective that contains the suffix *-able* or *-ible*.

1. A glass that is easy to <u>break</u> is _____.

2. Someone who has common <u>sense</u> is _____.

3. A structure that can be <u>collapsed</u> is _____.

4. An object that can be <u>collected</u> is _____.

5. Something that can be <u>eaten</u> is _____.

101

Does It Relate?

-al, -ial—suffixes meaning *relating to*

For each definition, write an adjective that uses the suffix *-al* or *-ial*.

1. _____: relating to colonies

2. _____: relating to nature

3. _____: relating to ethics

4. _____: relating to medicine

5. _____: relating to commerce

Daily Warm-Ups: Prefixes, Suffixes, & Roots

102

6. Now write a sentence using one of the adjectives above.

Suffix Meaning

Write a definition for each word on the line. Then answer the question that follows.

1. joyous: _____

2. courteous: _____

3. envious: _____

4. suspicious: _____

5. anxious: _____

6. What does the suffix *-ous* or *-eous* mean? _____

Daily Warm-Ups: Prefixes, Suffixes, & Roots

103

Make Me!

-ize—suffix meaning *make*

Make each of the underlined words below into a verb that uses the suffix *-ize*.

1. To create a <u>theory</u> is to _____.

2. To form a <u>union</u> is to _____.

3. To commit something to <u>memory</u> is to _____.

4. To make something <u>formal</u> is to _____.

5. To attribute the quality of being <u>ideal</u> is to _____.

104

What's It Made Of?

-en—suffix meaning *made of*

Write the correct word for each definition on the line.

1. _____: made of wood

2. _____: made of wool

3. _____: made of silk

4. _____: made of ash wood

5. Now use one of the words defined above in a sentence.

© 2006 Walch Publishing

State or Quality Of 1

-ion, -tion, -ation, -ition—suffixes meaning *state* or *quality of*

Complete each sentence below by making each of the underlined
words into a noun using one of the suffixes *-ion, -tion, -ation,* or *-ition.*

1. A person who <u>predicts</u> something makes a _____.

2. A person who is <u>indignant</u> is characterized by _____.

3. A person who is <u>inspired</u> has _____.

4. To <u>characterize</u> someone is to give him or her a _____.

5. To <u>imitate</u> an original is to create an _____.

106

6. Now think of other nouns that use one of these suffixes. Use one of them in
a sentence of your own.

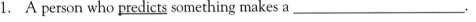
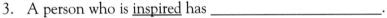

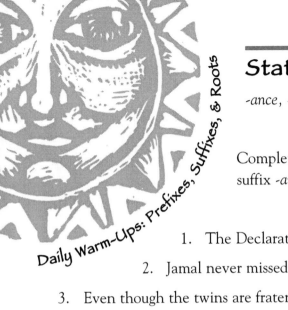

State or Act Of

-ance, -ence—suffixes meaning *state* or *act of*

Complete each sentence with a common noun that contains the suffix *-ance* or *-ence*.

1. The Declaration of _____ was signed in 1776.

2. Jamal never missed a day of school; his _____ was perfect.

3. Even though the twins are fraternal, they bear a striking _____ to each other.

4. Eva hates to wait for anything; she has very little _____.

5. Daniel prefers strawberry ice cream; his brother's _____ is for chocolate chip.

107

State, Act, or Condition Of

-hood, -ment, -ness, ship—suffixes meaning *state*, *act*, or *condition of*

Complete each sentence below by writing the correct suffix on
the line.

1. Tanya valued Amanda's friend_____ highly.

2. With embarass_____, Paul realized that he had poured salt, not sugar,
   into his coffee.

3. Dara's meticulous_____ makes her an excellent engineer.

4. We often visit friends in our old neighbor_____.

5. After he finished his lunch, Charlie leaned back in content_____.

108

What Does It Do? 1

The underlined words in the following sentences all contain the suffix -ly. Read each sentence, paying close attention to the underlined words. Then choose the correct phrase to complete the statement below.

The students <u>slowly</u> filed into the classroom.

We watched <u>wonderingly</u> as the magician performed her tricks.

The alarm clock rang <u>loudly</u> at five in the morning.

The suffix -ly turns

   a.   nouns into verbs.

   b.   verbs into adjectives.

   c.   adjectives into adverbs.

109

Describing People

Many suffixes describe people. Complete each sentence with the correct suffix. Write the suffix on the line.

1. Everybody smile while the photograph_____ takes your picture.

2. Jamie is a skilled music_____ who plays several different instruments.

3. A dedicated pian_____, he practices for hours every day.

4. As a visit_____ in another country, you can learn a great deal about a different culture.

5. As a teacher's assist_____, Mona helps to plan lessons.

110

Daily Warm-Ups: Prefixes, Suffixes, & Roots

Causing to Be

-en, -ify, -ize—suffixes meaning *to cause to be*

Complete each sentence with a verb that contains the suffix *-en*, *-ify, or -ize.* Use the clues in parentheses to help you.

1. Braiding the rope will _____ (make stronger) it.

2. The evidence will help the police _____ (discover the identity) their suspect.

3. This new invention will _____ (make revolutionary) the way people brush their teeth.

4. The witness will _____ (give testimony) after the court takes a brief recess.

5. The audience could not _____ (have sympathy for) with the movie's heroine.

111

State or Quality Of II

-ness, -y,-ity,- ty—suffixes meaning *state* or *quality of*

Complete each sentence with the correct suffix. Write the suffix on the line.

1. The cheering fans had great loyal_____ to their team, even when it was losing.

2. Dena hoped that with her new job would come prosper_____ for her family.

3. The whole school gathered together at the assembl_____.

4. A simple act of kind_____ can brighten someone's day immeasurably.

5. Due to the generos_____ of an anonymous donor, the school's basketball team has brand-new uniforms.

112

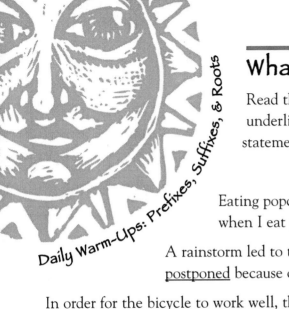

What Does It Do? II

Read the following sentences, paying close attention to the underlined words. Then choose the correct phrase to complete the statement.

Eating popcorn adds to my <u>enjoyment</u> of a movie. I <u>enjoy</u> movies more when I eat popcorn.

A rainstorm led to the <u>postponement</u> of the baseball game. The game was <u>postponed</u> because of the storm.

In order for the bicycle to work well, the wheels need to be in <u>alignment</u>. The bicycle's wheels must be <u>aligned</u> for it to work well.

The suffix *-ment* changes

    a. a verb to a noun.

    b. a noun to a verb.

    c. a noun to an adjective.

113

© 2006 Walch Publishing

Less Meaning

Read the following sentences, paying close attention to the underlined words. Then answer the question that follows.

She doesn't care about anyone's feelings. She is very <u>thoughtless</u>.

The drill is broken; it will be <u>useless</u> until it is fixed.

Miho would never lie to anyone. She is <u>guileless</u>.

What does the suffix *-less* mean? _____

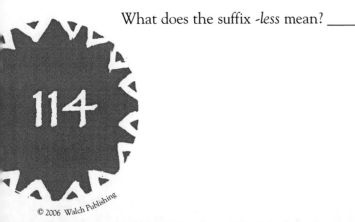

114

Which Way?

-ward—suffix meaning *direction*

Read the following definitions. Write the correct word containing the suffix *–ward* on the line.

1. _____ : direction going east

2. _____ : direction going up

3. _____ : direction going down

4. _____ : direction moving back

5. _____ : direction moving north

115

Full of What?

-ose—suffix meaning *full of*

Complete each sentence with a word from the box. Write the correct word on the line.

| verbose | morose | bellicose | lachrymose |

116

1. The essay is too _____; it needs to be edited so that it is less wordy.

2. Always _____, Angelo dissolved into tears anytime he saw a sad movie.

3. Although they have a reputation for being _____ dogs, most pit bulls are quite peaceful.

4. Unable to have things her own way, Gina pouted and felt _____.

5. Now use one of the words from the box in a sentence of your own.

Having a Tendency

-ile—suffix meaning *tending to* or *capable of*

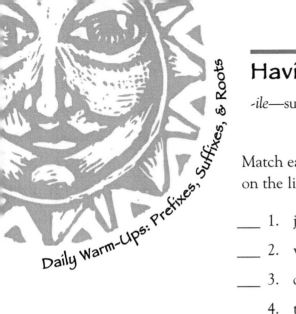

Daily Warm-Ups: Prefixes, Suffixes, & Roots

Match each word to its definition. Write the letter of the definition on the line.

___ 1. juvenile   a. calm, easy to manage

___ 2. volatile   b. relating to touch

___ 3. docile   c. explosive

___ 4. tactile   d. childish

5. Now use one of these *-ile* words in a sentence.

117

Something's Missing

Each of the following sentences is missing the same suffix. Complete the sentences by writing in the missing suffix. Then answer the questions that follow.

The project was shrouded in secre_____; only a few people knew anything about it.

The editor's job was to check the manuscripts for accura_____.

A curtain insured that people would have priva_____ while voting.

1. What is the missing suffix? _____

2. What does the suffix mean?

a. one who   b. state or quality of   c. doctrine, belief

State or Quality Of III

-ity—prefix meaning *state* or *quality of*

Complete the following sentences by changing each underlined adjective into a noun using the suffix *-ity*. Write the word on the line.

1. Something that is <u>necessary</u> is a _____.

2. People who are being <u>civil</u> are practicing _____.

3. Someone who is <u>creative</u> has a lot of _____.

4. People, being <u>mortal</u>, must face their own _____.

5. Somebody who is <u>credible</u> has _____.

119

I'm Inclined To . . .

-ive—suffix meaning *like, inclined to*

Write the correct word from the box next to each synonym.

active	talkative	expensive	expansive	pensive

1. costly _____

2. chatty _____

3. thoughtful _____

4. broad _____

5. lively _____

120

Circle the Suffix 1

Choose the correct suffix to complete each sentence. Circle the letter of the correct suffix.

1. When the crops did well, food was plenti_____ for the colonists.

   a. tude   b. ly   c. ful

2. The hikers gazed in wonder_____ at the waterfall.

   a. ful   b. ment   c. ing

3. The company held an annu_____ conference.

   a. al   b. ity   c. ness

4. When the restor_____ project is finished, the building will look exactly as it did in the middle of the nineteenth century.

   a. ation   b. ative   c. ment

5. The dinner will recogn_____ all of the volunteers who have worked with the organization this year.

   a. ize   b. ition   c. izable

121

Complete the Sentences

Each of the following sentences is missing the same suffix. Complete the sentences with the missing suffix. Then answer the questions that follow.

A person who lives someplace is a resid_____.

An overseeing administrator is a superintend_____.

A person who is not self-supporting is depend_____.

122

1. What is the missing suffix? _____

2. What does the suffix mean?

   a. tendency toward

   b. person who

   c. process of

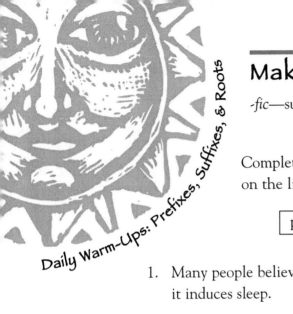

Making and Doing

-fic—suffix meaning *making, doing*

Complete each sentence with a word from the box. Write the word on the line.

prolific	scientific	terrific	soporific

1. Many people believe that chamomile has a _____ effect; it induces sleep.

2. A _____ artist produces a lot of work.

3. He combined work in the field and in the laboratory as part of his _____ research.

4. The car peeled away at a _____ speed.

5. Use one of the words in the box in a sentence of your own.

123

What Does It Resemble?

-ly—suffix meaning *resembling*

Complete each of the following sentences with a word that
contains the suffix *–ly*. Write the word on the line provided.

1. Someone who has the characteristics of a scholar is
   _____.

2. Someone who is like a mother is _____.

3. Someone who is similar to a brother is _____.

4. Someone who is matron-like is _____.

5. Someone who is like a grandfather is _____.

124

What's the State?

-tude—suffix meaning *state of*

Complete each sentence by changing the word in parentheses into a noun that ends in the suffix *-tude*. Write the word on the line.

1. She showed great _____ in her refusal to back down. (fortify)

2. The test showed that the student had a strong _____ for science. (apt)

3. Alone for the weekend at the lakeside cabin, she enjoyed the peace and _____. (solitary)

4. I sent a note expressing my _____ for all the help I had received. (grateful)

5. With _____, he answered each question on the test. (certain)

125

State or Quality Of IV

-or—suffix meaning *state* or *quality of*

Complete the sentences by replacing each word in parentheses with a noun using the suffix *-or*.

1. He always spoke with absolute (candid) _____.

2. Checking her homework, she found an (err) _____.

3. The audience was swept up in the (fervent) _____ of the speaker.

4. The soldier showed great (valiant) _____ in battle.

5. Nothing could match the (splendid) _____ of the fireworks display.

126

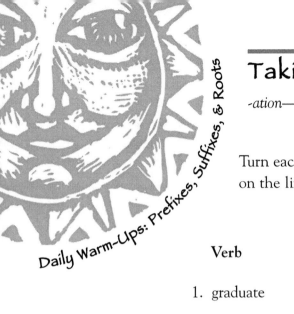

Taking Action

-ation—suffix meaning *action* or *process*

Turn each verb into a noun using the suffix *-ation*. Write the word on the line provided.

Verb	Noun
1. graduate	_____
2. educate	_____
3. imitate	_____
4. incline	_____
5. coronate	_____

127

6. Now use two of the –ation words above in sentences of your own.

Taking More Action

-ee—suffix meaning *recipient of action* or *performer of action*

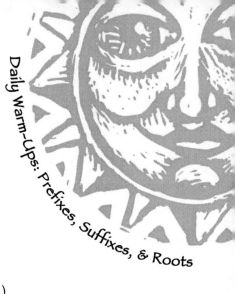

Complete each sentence with a word containing the suffix *-ee*. Use the underlined word to help you.

1. A person who is <u>employed</u> by someone is a(n) _____.

2. A person to whom something is legally <u>entrusted</u> is a(n) _____.

3. A person who is <u>absent</u> is a(n) _____.

4. A person who is <u>appointed</u> is a(n) _____.

5. Somebody who <u>attends</u> an event is a(n) _____.

6. Think of other words that contain the suffix *-ee*. List as many as you can.

128

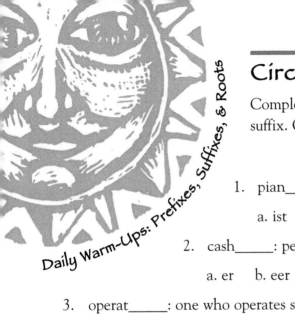

Circle the Suffix II

Complete the word for each definition by choosing the correct suffix. Circle the letter of the correct answer.

1. pian_____: person who plays the piano

   a. ist   b. eer   c. or

2. cash_____: person who works a cash register

   a. er   b. eer   c. ier

3. operat_____: one who operates something

   a. er   b. ar   c. or

4. li_____: one who lies

   a. er   b. ar   c. or

5. pion_____: one who leads the way

   a. eer   b. or   c. er

129

What Can You Make?

-ify—suffix meaning *to make*

Make each underlined noun into a verb by using the suffix *-ify*.
Write the word on the line.

1. To create <u>terror</u> is to _____.

2. To make something <u>false</u> is to _____.

3. To make something <u>beautiful</u> is to _____.

4. To make something have more <u>amplitude</u> is to _____.

5. To make something <u>pure</u> is to _____.

6. Now use one of the *-ify* words above in a sentence of your own.

130

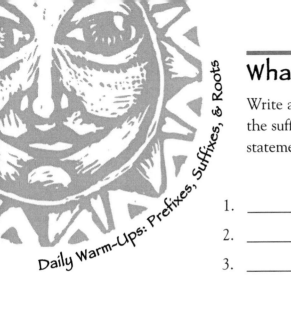

What Does It Do? III

Write a word for each definition by using the underlined word and the suffix *-al*. Then choose the correct phrase to complete the statement.

1. _____ : found in <u>nature</u>

2. _____ : having to do with a <u>tribe</u>

3. _____ : having to do with <u>paternity</u>

4. The suffix *-al*

   a. changes a noun to a verb.

   b. changes a verb to an adjective.

   c. changes a noun to an adjective.

131

© 2006 Walch Publishing

Suffixes

Why?

Complete each sentence with an adjective that combines the underlined word with the suffix -*y*. Then answer the question that follows.

1. Something containing a lot of <u>sugar</u> is _____.

2. Something covered with <u>dirt</u> is _____.

3. Someone who has a lot of <u>wealth</u> is _____.

4. What does the suffix -*y* mean?

   a. being or having

   b. person who

   c. place for

132

Daily Warm-Ups: Prefixes, Suffixes, & Roots

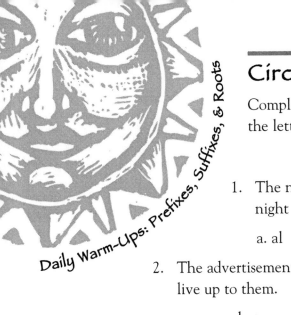

Circle the Suffix III

Complete each sentence by adding the appropriate suffix. Circle the letter of the correct answer.

1. The neighbors established a verb_____ agreement about late-night noise.

   a. al   b. ose   c. y

2. The advertisement made great claims, but in real_____ the product did not live up to them.

   a. ness   b. tor   c. ity

3. I find your whining to be very infant_____.

   a. ly   b. ile   c. ment

4. Eric is not a professional artist; he draws cartoons for his own amuse_____.

   a. ing   b. ment   c. ation

133

Daily Warm-Ups: Prefixes, Suffixes, & Roots

State or Quality Of V

-ation—suffix meaning *state* or *quality of*

Change each verb in parentheses to a noun that uses the suffix
-ation. Write the word on the line.

1. The new father looked at his baby with (adore)
   _____.

2. For these plants, the process of (mature) _____ takes
   only a few weeks.

3. As a painter, Carl often looks to nature for (inspire)
   _____.

4. Because we were at such a high (elevate) _____, it was
   difficult to breathe.

5. An (infest) _____ of insects ruined the crops.

134

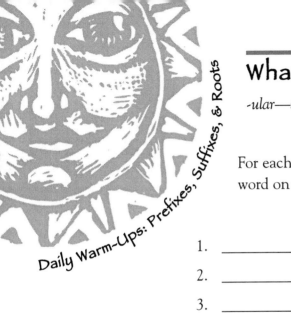

What Does It Relate To?

-ular—suffix meaning *relating to*

For each definition, write a term using the suffix *-ular*. Write the word on the line.

1. _____ : relating to cells

2. _____ : relating to a spectacle

3. _____ : relating to tubes

4. _____ : relating to circles

5. _____ : relating to rectangles

135

© 2006 Walch Publishing

Making Adjectives

Use a suffix to turn each word in parentheses into an adjective.
Write the adjective on the line.

1. The water was brown and foul-smelling; it was not (drink)
    _____.

2. After our long trip, we were happy to begin traveling (home)
    _____.

3. Thank you for the gift; it was very (thought) _____ of you.

4. Please arrange the files by (alphabet) _____ order.

5. Although Ella was born in America, her parents are (Vietnam)
    _____.

136

Making Verbs

Use a suffix to turn each word in parentheses into a verb. Write the verb on the line.

1. The storm is expected to (intense) _____ overnight.

2. Once you (priority) _____ your activities, you can decide how best to use your time.

3. Please (specific) _____ the size and color of the shirt you want.

4. We'll (category) _____ the documents according to the year in which they were written.

5. My speech will (emphasis) _____ our organization's accomplishments over the past year.

137

© 2006 Walch Publishing

How Strong?

Complete each sentence with the correct form of the word *strong* from the box below. Write the word on the line.

strongly	strengthen	strength	stronger

1. Gina does exercises to _____ her muscles.

2. I feel _____ that every person deserves a good education.

3. The wind is _____ than we had expected it to be.

4. With great _____, Pablo refused to act against his principles.

138

5. Now use one of the words from the box in a sentence of your own.

Daily Warm-Ups: Prefixes, Suffixes, & Roots

It's an Honor

Complete each sentence with the correct word from the box. Write the word on the line.

| honor | honorary | honorable | honorarium |

1. As a speaker at the dinner, he was paid an

   _____.

2. It was a great _____ to meet you.

3. While her intentions were _____, her actions sometimes belied her ideals.

4. Although the writer lacked formal schooling, the college eventually granted him an _____ degree for his literary contributions.

139

5. Now use one of the words from the box in a sentence of your own.

Making Nouns

Use a suffix to turn each word in parentheses into a noun. Write the noun on the line.

1. With (free) _____ comes a great deal of responsibility.

2. Each spring you can witness the birds' (migrate) _____ back to the north.

3. I always ask for the librarian's (recommend) _____ when I'm looking for a new book to read.

4. We are in (agree) _____ about most issues.

5. Imagine my surprise at the (realize) _____ that my neighbors are distant relatives of mine.

140

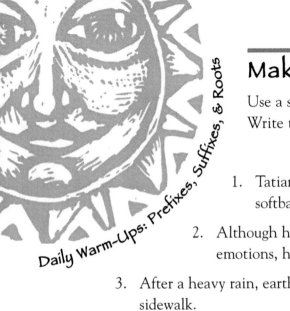

Making More Adjectives

Use a suffix to turn each word in parentheses into an adjective.
Write the adjective on the line.

1. Tatiana is the most (power) _____ pitcher on the softball team.

2. Although he is not (demonstrate) _____ with his emotions, he has strong feelings.

3. After a heavy rain, earthworms are (plenty) _____ on the sidewalk.

4. Normally brave, Paul got (panic) _____ at the thought of riding on a roller coaster.

5. His story was so absurd that it was barely (believe) _____.

141

Daily Warm-Ups: Prefixes, Suffixes, & Roots

Matching Suffixes

Match each word to its definition. Write the letter of the definition on the line.

____ 1. accuse

____ 2. accusation

____ 3. accuser

____ 4. accusatory

a. a charge of wrongdoing

b. to charge with wrongdoing

c. implying or expressing wrongdoing

d. one who makes a charge of wrongdoing

5. Now use one of the above words in a sentence of your own.

142

Make It Complete

Complete each sentence with the correct suffix. Write the suffix on the line.

1. The goal of our committee is to beauti_____ the neighborhood.

2. The new flowers we planted are quite beauti_____.

3. Our group meets week_____ to discuss our plans.

4. We've met with obstacles, but they only fort_____ our resolve.

5. We consider ourselves fortun_____ to have the support of the townspeople.

143

Suffixes

What's in the Box?

Complete each sentence with the correct word from the box.
Write the word on the line.

| dictate | dictator | dictation | diction | dictionary |

1. Ben types quickly and is good at transcribing _____.

2. Italy, once under the rule of a _____, now has a
   parliamentary system of government.

3. While Alice reads and writes like a native speaker of English, her
   _____ needs improvement.

4. A good _____ gives not only a word's definition, but its origin
   and pronunciation.

5. The club's bylaws _____ that a new president be elected every
   two years.

144

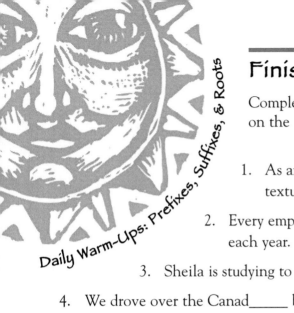

Finish It!

Complete each sentence with the correct suffix. Write the suffix on the line.

1. As an art_____, Henry experiments with different colors and textures in his paintings.

2. Every employ_____ in the company receives two weeks of vacation each year.

3. Sheila is studying to be an engin_____ who designs bridges.

4. We drove over the Canad_____ border on our way to the lake.

5. Emma is a professional opera sing_____ who has performed all over the world.

145

© 2006 Walch Publishing

A Person Who . . .

Complete each word with the correct suffix. Use the definitions to help you.

1. employ_____: a person who hires workers

2. attend_____: a person who attends

3. cell_____: a person who plays the cello

4. decorat_____: a person who decorates

5. auction_____: a person who runs an auction

146

6. Now use one of these words in a sentence of your own.

Daily Warm-Ups: Prefixes, Suffixes, & Roots

Adjective Suffix

Read the following definitions. Write the word that fits each definition on the line. Each word should be an adjective that contains the suffix *-ive*.

1. _____: costing a lot

2. _____: having the ability to create

3. _____: opposite of positive

4. _____: very large

5. _____: thoughtful

6. Now write a sentence using an *-ive* word.

147

Another Adjective Suffix

Read the following definitions. Write the word that fits each
definition on the line. Each word should be an adjective that
contains the suffix *-ic*.

1. _____: mysterious

2. _____: simple

3. _____: relating to what is real

4. _____: taking place in the past

5. Now write a sentence using an *-ic* word.

148

Daily Warm-Ups: Prefixes, Suffixes, & Roots

Noun Suffix

Read the following definitions. Write the word that fits each definition on the line. Each word should be a noun that contains the suffix *-sion*.

1. _____ : the act of admitting

2. _____ : the act or process of deciding

3. _____ : the act of concluding

4. _____ : a feeling of being tense

5. _____ : the act of propelling

6. Now write a sentence using a *-sion* word.

149

© 2006 Walch Publishing

Verb Suffix

Read the following definitions. Write the word that fits each definition on the line. Each word should be a verb that contains the suffix -*ate*.

1. _____: to oversee the rules of a game

2. _____: to remove by cutting

3. _____: to set free

4. _____: to copy

5. _____: to threaten; to create fear

6. Now write a sentence using an -*ate* word.

150

Just My Luck!

Each word below contains the root *fortu*, meaning *luck* or *chance*. Use your knowledge of prefixes and suffixes to write a definition for each word.

1. fortunate

   _____

2. misfortune

   _____

3. fortuitous

   _____

4. unfortunately

   _____

5. fortune

   _____

151

Say What?

Each word below contains the root *dic*, which means *say*. Use your knowledge of prefixes and suffixes to match each word to its definition. Write the letter of the correct definition on the line.

___ 1. predict

___ 2. dictator

___ 3. malediction

___ 4. contradict

a. to speak against; to say the opposite

b. one who dictates; one with complete power

c. to say in advance

d. a curse

5. Use one of the words above in a sentence of your own.

152

Opposites Attract

Use your knowledge of prefixes and suffixes to choose the *opposite* of each word. Circle the letter of the correct answer.

1. just

   a. adjust   b. unjust   c. justice

2. artful

   a. artless   b. artist   c. artistic

3. capable

   a. capability   b. incapability   c. incapable

4. natural

   a. nature   b. unnatural   c. unnaturally

5. active

   a. reactive   b. activity   c. inactive

153

© 2006 Walch Publishing

That's Poisonous!

The following words contain the root *tox*, which means *poison*.
Use your knowledge of prefixes and suffixes to match each word to
its definition.

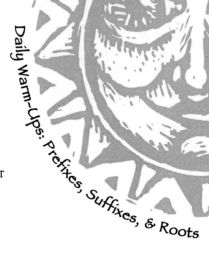

___ 1. toxic

___ 2. antitoxin

___ 3. toxin

___ 4. nontoxic

a. not poisonous

b. something that works against, or
counteracts, a toxin

c. poisonous substance

d. poisonous

5. Now use one of the words above in a sentence of your own.

154

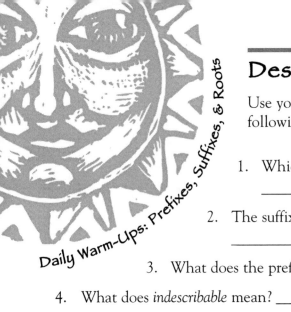

Describe It!

Use your knowledge of roots, prefixes, and suffixes to answer the following questions about the word *indescribable*.

1. Which part of the word is the root that means *write*?

   _____

2. The suffix *-able* signals that the word is what part of speech?

   _____

3. What does the prefix *in-* mean? _____

4. What does *indescribable* mean? _____

5. Use the word *indescribable* in a sentence.

Daily Warm-Ups: Prefixes, Suffixes, & Roots

155

It's a Mystery!

Use your knowledge of prefixes, suffixes, and roots to answer the following questions about the word *demystifiy*.

1. Which part of the word is the root that means *mystery*?

   _____

2. The suffix *-ify* signals that the word is what part of speech?

   _____

3. What does the prefix *de-* mean? _____

4. What does *demystify* mean? _____

5. Use the word *demystify* in a sentence.

156

What's a Precursor?

Use your knowledge of prefixes, suffixes, and roots to answer the following questions about the word *precursor*.

1. Which part of the word is the root that means *run*?

   _____

2. What does the prefix *pre-* mean? _____

3. The suffix *-or* signals that the word is what part of speech?

   _____

4. What does *precursor* mean? _____

5. Use the word *precursor* in a sentence.

157

Rage

The following words are based on the root *fur*, which means *rage*. Use your knowledge of prefixes and suffixes to match each word to its meaning. Write the letter of the correct answer on the line.

___ 1. furious

___ 2. infuriating

___ 3. furiously

___ 4. fury

a. anger

b. causing anger

c. angrily

d. angry

5. Use one of the words from the left-hand column in a sentence of your own.

158

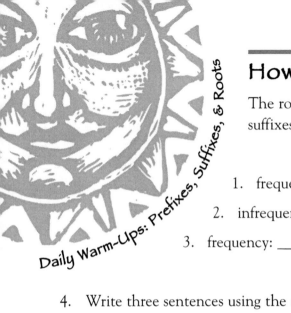

How Often?

The root *freq* means *often*. Use your knowledge of prefixes and suffixes to write a definition for each word.

1. frequent: _____

2. infrequent: _____

3. frequency: _____

4. Write three sentences using the above words.

At an End

The following words are based on the root *fin*, which means *end*.
Use your knowledge of prefixes and suffixes to write a definition
for each word.

1. finite: _____

2. infinite: _____

3. final: _____

160

4. Write three sentences using the above words.

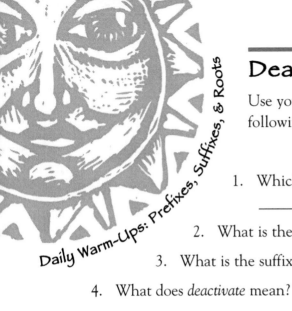

Deactivate

Use your knowledge of prefixes, suffixes, and roots to answer the following questions about the word *deactivate*.

1. Which part of the word is the root that means *to drive, to do*?

    _____

2. What is the prefix that means *not, opposite*? _____

3. What is the suffix that indicates that the word is a verb? _____

4. What does *deactivate* mean?

    _____

5. Use the word *deactivate* in a sentence.

161

I Don't Believe It!

Use your knowledge of prefixes and suffixes to write the correct word for each definition. Each answer should be a variation of the word *belief*.

1. _____: (adj) able to be believed

2. _____: (adj) not able to be believed

3. _____: (noun) lack of belief

4. _____: (noun) one who believes

5. Use one of the words above in a sentence of your own.

162

Improbable

Use your knowledge of prefixes, suffixes, and roots to answer the following questions about the word *improbable*.

1. *Improbable* is the opposite of

   a. babble.   b. probable.   c. problem.

2. The suffix that indicates that the word is an adjective is _____.

3. A synonym for *improbable* is

   a. unlikely.   b. uninteresting.   c. undecided.

4. Use the word *improbable* in a sentence of your own.

163

Always a Critic

Use your knowledge of prefixes and suffixes to match each word to its definition. Write the letter of the definition on the line.

____ 1. critic

____ 2. critical

____ 3. criticism

____ 4. uncritical

a. judgmental

b. one who analyzes or judges

c. judgment or analysis

d. not analyzing or judging

5. Use one of the above words in a sentence.

164

Flying Solo

Use your knowledge of prefixes, suffixes, and roots to answer the following questions.

1. The words *sole*, *solo*, *solitary*, and *desolate* are all based on the root _____.

2. The root means

   a. several.

   b. wisdom.

   c. alone.

3. Another word containing this root is _____.

4. Use one of the words containing this root in a sentence.

Daily Warm-Ups: Prefixes, Suffixes, & Roots

165

Trembling

Use your knowledge of prefixes, suffixes, and roots to answer the following questions.

1. The words *tremor, tremulous,* and *tremble* are all based on the root _____.

2. The root means

   a. quake. b. welcome. c. try.

3. The word *trembling* means _____.

4. Use one of the words containing this root in a sentence.

166

Daily Warm-Ups: Prefixes, Suffixes, & Roots

Try Again

Use your knowledge of roots and prefixes to match the following words with their definitions. Each word is based on the root *tempt*, which means *try*.

_____ 1. attempt   a. enticing

_____ 2. reattempt   b. able to be tempted

_____ 3. temptation   c. try again

_____ 4. tempting   d. try

_____ 5. temptable   e. something that is enticing

6. Use one of the words above in a sentence of your own.

167

Doing Well

Use your knowledge of roots and prefixes to match the following words with their definitions. Each word is based on the root *bene*, which means *well*.

___ 1. unbeneficial   a. one who helps

___ 2. benefit   b. not helpful

___ 3. benevolent   c. doing good

___ 4. benefactor   d. help

5. Use one of the words from the left-hand column in a sentence.

168

In a Week

Use your knowledge of prefixes, suffixes, and roots to answer the following questions about the word *biweekly*.

1. Which part of the word *biweekly* is the root? _____

2. What is the prefix that means *two*? _____

3. The suffix *-ly* indicates that *biweekly* is what part of speech?

   a. adjective

   b. adverb

   c. verb

4. Use the word *biweekly* in a sentence.

169

Daily Warm-Ups: Prefixes, Suffixes, & Roots

In This Skin

Use your knowledge of prefixes and suffixes to match each word to its definition. Each word is based on the root *derm*, which means *skin*.

___ 1. dermatologist

___ 2. epidermis

___ 3. dermal

___ 4. dermatology

a. relating to skin

b. branch of science dealing with the skin

c. outside layer of skin

d. doctor who treats skin

170

5. Use one of the words from the left-hand column in a sentence.

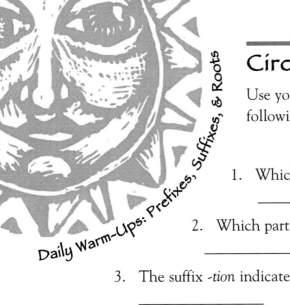

Circumspection

Use your knowledge of prefixes, suffixes, and roots to answer the following questions about the word *circumspection*.

1. Which part of the word is the root meaning *to see*?

   _____

2. Which part of the word is the prefix meaning *around*?

   _____

3. The suffix *-tion* indicates that the word is what part of speech?

   _____

4. What does *circumspection* mean? _____

5. Use the word *circumspection* in a sentence.

© 2006 Walch Publishing

What Time?

Use your knowledge of prefixes, suffixes, and roots to answer the questions about the words in the box below.

| chronic   chronology   synchronize |

1. What root, meaning *time*, does each word contain?

   _____

2. Which word contains a prefix meaning *together*? _____

3. Which word is an adjective? _____

4. Use one of the words from the box in a sentence.

172

Rejuvenating

Use your knowledge of prefixes, suffixes, and roots to answer the following questions about the word *rejuvenate*.

1. What part of the word is the root meaning *youth*?

   a. rejuv   b. venate   c. juven

2. What is the prefix meaning *again*?

   a. rejuv-   b. rejuven-   c. re-

3. What is the suffix that indicates the word is a verb?

   a. -venate   b. -nate   c. -ate

4. What does *rejuvenate* mean?

   a. to make youthful again

   b. to remember one's youth again

   c. to behave childishly again

5. Now use rejuvenate in a sentence of your own.

173

Labor-Intensive

Use your knowledge of prefixes, suffixes, and roots to match each word to its definition.

____ 1. labor

____ 2. laboratory

____ 3. collaborate

____ 4. laborer

a. place where work, usually scientific, is done

b. one who works

c. work together

d. work

5. Use one of the words from the left-hand column in a sentence.

174

Daily Warm-Ups: Prefixes, Suffixes, & Roots

Stronger

Use your knowledge of prefixes, suffixes, and roots to choose the correct word from the box for each definition. Write the word on the line. Each word in the box is based on the root *fort*, which means *strong*.

refortification	fortress	fortitude	fortify

1. _____ : strength

2. _____ : stronghold

3. _____ : strengthen

4. _____ : strengthening again

5. Now use one of the words from the box in a sentence of your own.

175

Write Now

Use your knowledge of prefixes, suffixes, and roots to choose the correct word from the box for each definition. Write the word on the line. Each word is based on the root *scrib*, which means *write*.

scribe	scribble	inscribe	circumscribe

1. _____: to write on or engrave

2. _____: to draw a line around

3. _____: one who writes

4. _____: to write carelessly

5. Now use one of the words from the box in a sentence.

176

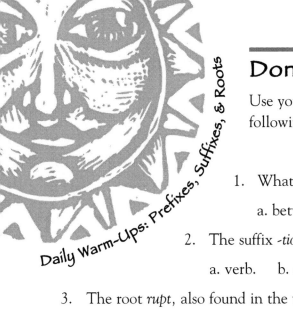

Don't Interrupt Me!

Use your knowledge of prefixes, suffixes, and roots to answer the following questions about the word *interruption*.

1. What does the prefix *inter* mean?

    a. between   b. before   c. again

2. The suffix *-tion* indicates that the word is a(n)

    a. verb.   b. noun.   c. adjective.

3. The root *rupt*, also found in the words *rupture* and *erupt*, means

    a. see.   b. speak.   c. break.

4. Use the word *interruption* in a sentence.

177

© 2006 Walch Publishing

It's a Go!

Use your knowledge of prefixes and suffixes to create words based on the root *gress*, which means *go*.

1. To move forward is to _____gress.

2. A violation of the law is a transgress_____.

3. To move backward is to _____gress.

4. Somebody who is very forceful is agress_____.

5. A forward movement is a _____gress_____.

6. Now write a sentence using one of the words above.

178

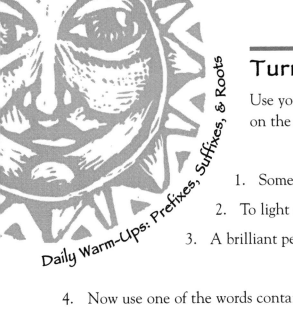

Turn on the Light!

Use your knowledge of prefixes and suffixes to create words based on the root *lum*, which means *light*.

1. Something that shines brightly is lumin_____.

2. To light something up is to _____luminate it.

3. A brilliant person is a lumin_____.

4. Now use one of the words containing the root *lumin* in a sentence.

179

Living

Use your knowledge of prefixes and suffixes to create words based on the root *vit*, which means *to live*.

1. Something necessary to life is vit_____.

2. If you breathe new life into something you _____vitalize it.

3. Somebody who is lively is full of vital_____.

4. Now use one of the words containing the root *vit* in a sentence.

180

1. 1. acrimonious, 2. acidity, 3. acrid, 4. acerbic
2. 1. *ag*, 2. to move, to do
3. 1. a, 2. b, 3. a
4. 1. *dent*, 2. *card*, 3. *ped*, 4. *man*, 5. *psych*, 6. heart, 7. tooth, 8. hand, 9. foot, 10. brain
5. 1. democracy, 2. monarchy, 3. aristocracy, 4. oligarchy, 5. Sentences will vary.
6. 1. *loqu*, 2. *loqu*, 3. *locut*, 4. *loqu*, 5. *locut*, 6. Words will vary.
7. 1. d, 2. a, 3. b, 4. e, 5. c
8. 1. factory, 2. fiction, 3. infected, 4. effect, 5. affect
9. 1. *cent*, 2. *milli*, 3. *dec*, 4. *cent*, 5. *dec*
10. 1. voc, 2. voice, call
11. 1. *geo*, 2. *herbi*, 3. *hydro*, 4. *photo*, 5. *aero*, 6. *aero*—relating to air; *geo*—relating to the earth; *herbi*—relating to plants; *hydro*—relating to water; *photo*—relating to light
12. 1. prenatal, 2. native, 3. international, 4. supernatural, 5. naturalized
13. 1. e, 2. f, 3. c, 4. a, 5. d, 6. b
14. 1. nondescript, 2. transcribe, 3. inscription,

4. postscript, 5. scribble, 6. The roots mean *to write.*
15. 1. d, 2. a, 3. e, 4. b, 5. c
16. 1. November, 2. heptagon, 3. quintuplet, 4. October, 5. hexagon
17. 1. hemi, 2. semi, 3. semi, 4. demi, 5. *Semi, hemi,* and *demi* all mean *half.*
18. 1. b, 2. c, 3. a, 4. d, 5. e
19. 1. a, 2. b, 3. a
20. 1–4. *morph*, 5. shape, form
21. 1. d, 2. c, 3. b, 4. a, 5. a
22. 1. a, 2. d, 3. e, 4. c, 5. b
23. 1–4. *lum*, 5. light
24. 1. elaborate, 2. collaborate, 3. laboratory, 4. labor, 5. *labor*, 6. to work
25. 1. conjunction, 2. junction, 3. juncture, 4. injunction
26. 1. audience, 2. audible, 3. auditorium, 4. audition, 5. audiovisual
27. 1. b, 2. Sentences will vary.
28. 1–5. *port*, 6. b

Daily Warm-Ups: Prefixes, Suffixes, & Roots

29.   1. d, 2. c, 3. b, 4. a
30.   1. thermometer, 2. thermos, 3. thermostat,
      4. *therm*, 5. heat
31.   1. *vict*, 2. *vanq*, 3. *vinc*, 4. *vict*, 5. *vinc*, 6. *vict*
32.   1. misplaced in time, 2. time line, 3. set to the
      same time, 4. by time of occurrence
33.   1. documents, 2. recognizing, 3. cognition,
      4. indoctrination, 5. docile
34.   1. newness, 2. beginning, new, 3. fresh, new,
      4. new
35.   1. d, 2. e, 3. b, 4. a, 5. c, 6. water
36.   1. a, 2. b, 3. c, 4. b
37.   1. *fin*, 2. end
38.   1. skin, 2. blood, 3. bone
39.   1. citizen, 2. civil, 3. civilization, 4. civic,
      5. civilian
40.   1. zoologist, 2. botany, 3. zoology, 4. zoo,
      5. botanical, 6. botanist
41.   1. basement, 2. altitude, 3. basics, 4. exalted,
      5. bass

42.   1. e, 2. a, 3. d, 4. c, 5. b
43.   1. current, 2. excursion, 3. precursor, 4. cursory,
      5. occur
44.   1. journal, 2. journey, 3. nocturnal, 4. adjourn
45.   1. stretched out, 2. persistent, 3. tautness,
      4. inclination, habit
46.   1. speed up, 2. speed, 3. slow down
47.   1. fragile, 2. infraction, 3. fracture, 4. fragment,
      5. fraction
48.   1. b, 2. a, 3. c, 4. b
49.   1. set free, 2. freedom, 3. generously; freely, 4. free
50.   1. commute, 2. permutation, 3. mutate,
      4. immutable
51.   1. *ir*, 2. *in*, 3. *il*, 4. *in*, 5. *im*
52.   1. amoral, 2. atypical, 3. asymmetrical, 4. atonal,
      5. achromatic, 6. Sentences will vary.
53.   Answers may vary. 1. unwilling, 2. unhappy,
      3. unoriginal, 4. uneven, 5. unmet
54.   1. c, 2. d, 3. e, 4. a, 5. b, 6. Sentences will vary.
55.   1. *in*, 2. *un*, 3. *in*, 4. *il*, 5. *a*, 6. *dis*

Daily Warm-Ups: Prefixes, Suffixes, & Roots

56. 1. against bacteria, 2. opposite, 3. dislike, 4. against, opposite
57. 1. *en*, 2. *em*, 3. *en*, 4. *en*, 5. *em*
58. 1. diagram, 2. diameter, 3. diagonal, 4. dialogue, 5. diagnose
59. Answers may vary. 1. costing too much, 2. thought too highly of, 3. exaggerated, stated too strongly, 4. not appreciated enough, 5. not estimated highly enough, 6. not cooked enough
60. 1. b, 2. a, 3. b, 4. c, 5. above, high, 6. beneath, low
61. 1. d, 2. c, 3. a, 4. b
62. 1. *pre*, 2. *re*, 3. *post*, 4. *pre*, 5. *re*
63. 1. empower, 2. ennoble, 3. enrage, 4. embitter, 5. enlarge, 6. Words will vary.
64. 1. immerse, 2. induce, 3. impress, inhale
65. 1–4. *non-*, 5. not
66. c
67. 1. affix, 2. aboard, 3. ashore, 4. afoot, 5. b
68. 1. extraterrestrial, 2. extracurricular, 3. extraordinary, 4. extrovert, 5. extravagant

69. 1. d, 2. c, 3. a, 4. b
70. 1. b, 2. c, 3. a, 4. involving change
71. 1. *olig*, 2. *mono*, 3. *multi*, 4. *mono*, 5. *multi*
72. 1. spread through, 2. not allowing anything to pass through, 3. convince, 4. appropriate to, having to do with
73. 1. *sys*, 2. *syn*, 3. *syl*, 4. *sym*, 5. *syn*, 6. *sym*
74. 1. d, 2. c, 3. a, 4. b
75. c
76. 1. false name, 2. methodology that is not scientific (false science), 3. not really classic (falsely classic)
77. a
78. 1. separate, 2. seclusion, 3. secession, 4. segregate, 5. secede
79. 1. parallel, 2. parachute, 3. paraphrase, 4. paradox, 5. paragraph
80. 1. abscond, 2. abhor, 3. absent, 4. abstract, 5. abstain
81. 1. *un*, 2. *ir*, 3. *non*, 4. *dis*, 5. *de*
82. 1. adventure, 2. advert, 3. admit, 4. adorn,

Daily Warm-Ups: Prefixes, Suffixes, & Roots

    5. adjacent

83. b
84. 1. c, 2. a, 3. b, 4. d, 5. e
85. a
86. 1. vice president, 2. vice principal, 3. vice admiral, 4. vice chairman
87. 1. c, 2. e, 3. b, 4. d, 5. a
88. 1. dyslexia, 2. dyspepsia, 3. dysfunction, 4. dystopia, 5. dysphonia
89. 1. b, 2. c, 3. a, 4. d, 5. Sentences will vary.
90. a
91. 1. d, 2. a, 3. b, 4. c
92. 1. deemphasizing, 2. decreased, 3. deflate, 4. decontaminated, 5. decelerating
93. 1. c, 2. a, 3. b, 4. a, 5. c
94. 1. b, 2. a, 3. c, 4. c, 5. a
95. 1. *a*, 2. *pro*, 3. *tele*, 4. *post*, 5. *magni*
96. 1. c, 2. b, 3. b, 4. b, 5. c
97. 1. c, 2. b, 3. c, 4. b, 5. a
98. 1. c, 2. b, 3. a, 4. d, 5. Sentences will vary.

99. 1. d, 2. c, 3. b, 4. a, 5. e, 6. Words will vary.
100. 1. b, 2. d, 3. a, 4. c, 5. e, 6. Words will vary.
101. 1. breakable, 2. sensible, 3. collapsible, 4. collectable or collectible, 5. edible
102. 1. colonial, 2. natural, 3. ethical, 4. medicinal, 5. commercial, 6. Sentences will vary.
103. 1. full of joy, 2. full of courtesy, 3. full of envy, 4. full of suspicion, 5. full of anxiety, 6. full of
104. 1. theorize, 2. unionize, 3. memorize, 4. formalize, 5. idealize
105. 1. wooden, 2. woolen, 3. silken, 4. ashen 5. Sentences will vary.
106. 1. prediction, 2. indignation, 3. inspiration, 4. characterization, 5. imitation, 6. Sentences will vary.
107. 1. Independence, 2. attendance, 3. resemblance, 4. patience, 5. preference
108. 1. *ship*, 2. *ment*, 3. *ness*, 4. *hood*, 5. *ment*
109. c
110. 1. *er*, 2. *ian*, 3. *ist*, 4. *or*, 5. *ant*

111. 1. strengthen, 2. identify, 3. revolutionize, 4. testify, 5. sympathize
112. 1. *ty*, 2. *ity*, 3. *y*, 4. *ness*, 5. *ity*
113. a
114. without
115. 1. eastward, 2. upward, 3. downward, 4. backward, 5. northward
116. 1. verbose, 2. lachrymose, 3. bellicose, 4. morose, 5. Sentences will vary.
117. 1. d, 2. c, 3. a, 4. b, 5. Sentences will vary.
118. 1. *-cy*, 2. b
119. 1. necessity, 2. civility, 3. creativity, 4. mortality, 5. credibility
120. 1. expensive, 2. talkative, 3. pensive, 4. expansive, 5. active
121. 1. c, 2. b, 3. a, 4. a, 5. a
122. 1. *-ent*, 2. b
123. 1. soporific, 2. prolific, 3. scientific, 4. terrific, 5. Sentences will vary.
124. 1. scholarly, 2. motherly, 3. brotherly, 4. matronly, 5. grandfatherly

125. 1. fortitude, 2. aptitude, 3. solitude, 4. gratitude, 5. certitude
126. 1. candor, 2. error, 3. fervor, 4. valor, 5. splendor
127. 1. graduation, 2. education, 3. imitation, 4. inclination, 5. coronation, 6. Sentences will vary.
128. 1. employee, 2. trustee, 3. absentee, 4. appointee, 5. attendee, 6. Words will vary.
129. 1. a, 2. c, 3. c, 4. b, 5. a
130. 1. terrify, 2. falsify, 3. beautify, 4. amplify, 5. purify, 6. Sentences will vary.
131. 1. natural, 2. tribal, 3. paternal, 4. c
132. 1. sugary, 2. dirty, 3. wealthy, 4. a
133. 1. a, 2. c, 3. b, 4. b
134. 1. adoration, 2. maturation, 3. inspiration, 4. elevation, 5. infestation
135. 1. cellular, 2. spectacular, 3. tubular, 4. circular, 5. rectangular
136. 1. drinkable, 2. homeward, 3. thoughtful, 4. alphabetical, 5. Vietnamese
137. 1. intensify, 2. prioritize, 3. specify, 4. categorize,

5. emphasize
138. 1. strengthen, 2. strongly, 3. stronger, 4. strength, 5. Sentences will vary.
139. 1. honorarium, 2. honor, 3. honorable, 4. honorary, 5. Sentences will vary.
140. 1. freedom, 2. migration, 3. recommendation, 4. agreement, 5. realization
141. 1. powerful, 2. demonstrative, 3. plentiful, 4. panicky, 5. believable
142. 1. b, 2. a, 3. d, 4. c, 5. Sentences will vary.
143. 1. *fy*, 2. *ful*, 3. *ly*, 4. *ify*, 5. *ate*
144. 1. dictation, 2. dictator, 3. diction, 4. dictionary, 5. dictate
145. 1. *ist*, 2. *ee*, 3. *eer*, 4. *ian*, 5. *er*
146. 1. *er*, 2. *ee*, 3. *ist*, 4. *or*, 5. *eer*
147. Answers may vary. 1. expensive, 2. creative, 3. negative, 4. massive, 5. pensive, 6. Sentences will vary.
148. Answers may vary. 1. cryptic, 2. basic, 3. realistic, 4. historic, 5. Sentences will vary.

149. 1. admission, 2. decision, 3. conclusion, 4. tension, 5. propulsion, 6. Sentences will vary.
150. Answers may vary. 1. officiate, 2. amputate, 3. liberate, 4. imitate, 5. intimidate, 6. Sentences will vary.
151. 1. lucky, 2. bad luck, 3. occurring by luck, 4. unluckily, 5. luck, chance, wealth
152. 1. c, 2. b, 3. d, 4. a, 5. Sentences will vary.
153. 1. b, 2. a, 3. c, 4. b, 5. c
154. 1. d, 2. b, 3. c, 4. d, 5. Sentences will vary.
155. 1. *scrib*, 2. adjective, 3. not, 4. unable to be described, 5. Sentences will vary.
156. 1. *myst*, 2. verb, 3. reverse, opposite, 4. to make something not mysterious; to take the mystery out of something, 5. Sentences will vary.
157. 1. *cur*, 2. before, 3. noun, 4. something that came before; forerunner, 5. Sentences will vary.
158. 1. d, 2. b, 3. c, 4. a, 5. Sentences will vary.
159. 1. often, 2. not often, 3. number of times; state of occurring often, 4. Sentences will vary.

160. 1. having an end or limits, 2. without an end or limits, 3. last, 4. Sentences will vary.
161. 1. *act*, 2. *de-*, 3. *-ate*, 4. to make inactive, 5. Sentences will vary.
162. 1. believable, 2. unbelievable, 3. disbelief, 4. believer, 5. Sentences will vary.
163. 1. b, 2. *-able*, 3. a, 4. Sentences will vary.
164. 1. b, 2. a, 3. c, 4. d, 5. Sentences will vary.
165. 1. *sol*, 2. c, 3. Answers will vary. 4. Sentences will vary.
166. 1. *trem*, 2. a, 3. shaking, 4. Sentences will vary.
167. 1. d, 2. c, 3. e, 4. a, 5. b, 6. Sentences will vary.
168. 1. b, 2. d, 3. c, 4. a, 5. Sentences will vary.
169. 1. week, 2. *bi*, 3. b, 4. Sentences will vary.
170. 1. d, 2. c, 3. a, 4. b, 5. Sentences will vary.
171. 1. *spect*, 2. *circum*, 3. noun, 4. the act of looking around, 5. Sentences will vary.
172. 1. *chron*, 2. synchronize, 3. chronic, 4. Sentences will vary.
173. 1. c, 2. c, 3. c, 4. a, 5. Sentences will vary.

174. 1. d, 2. a, 3. c, 4. b, 5. Sentences will vary.
175. 1. fortitude, 2. fortress, 3. fortify, 4. refortification, 5. Sentences will vary.
176. 1. inscribe, 2. circumscribe, 3. scribe, 4. scribble, 5. Sentences will vary.
177. 1. a, 2. b, 3. c, 4. Sentences will vary.
178. 1. *pro*, 2. *ion*, 3. *re*, 4. *ive*, 5. *pro, ion*, 6. Sentences will vary.
179. 1. *ous*, 2. *il*, 3. *ary*, 4. Sentences will vary.
180. 1. *al*, 2. *re*, 3. *ity*, 4. Sentences will vary.

Turn downtime into learning time!

For information on other titles in the

Daily *Warm-Ups* series,

visit our web site: walch.com